Trial

TRIAL
by
Tom Hayden

Thomas Hayden

JONATHAN CAPE
THIRTY BEDFORD SQUARE
LONDON

First published in Great Britain 1971
© 1970 by Tom Hayden

Jonathan Cape Ltd, 30 Bedford Square, London WC1

Hardback edition ISBN 0 224 00521 9
Paperback edition ISBN 0 224 00553 7

Printed and bound in Great Britain
by Butler & Tanner Ltd, Frome and London

Contents

Trial

INTRODUCTION

A few nights before the trial began, the defendants, the legal staff, and our attorneys were sitting around a suburban Chicago living room, together with Fred Hampton and Bobby Rush of the Illinois Black Panthers, arguing about violence. Demonstrations were on the agenda for September 24, the opening day of the trial, and again in mid-October, the latter having been called by the Weathermen. The Panthers were opposed to street violence as planned by the white revolutionaries of SDS. They wanted a disciplined and orderly show of support for their chairman, Bobby Seale, our fellow defendant who was already in jail. Who were these white kids anyway, they asked, planning to run wild in the streets? Did they need to learn something new about the brutality of the Chicago police? Who was going to be mobilized by these actions? Violence should be used in defense—self-defense—when the police attacked programs which the community supported.

I disagreed fundamentally with Weathermen politics, which emphasized violence and identification with the Third World as a substitute for organizing a mass movement among whites in the United States. But I thought it would be politically destructive for the Panthers to condemn publicly the proposed street action. If anything, most white radicals were too soft, as the Weathermen charged, not too militant. Why should the Panthers or the Conspiracy put the clamps on the rising spirit of militancy among students and young people?

The arguments went on in our heads after that evening and resumed a few days later at the Conspiracy office. Bobby Rush then took command of the discussion and brought the issues to a climax, emphasizing that we were not taking either the demonstrations or the trial seriously enough. We didn't realize how much everything mattered now, he said, how rapidly the government was moving toward fascism, and how our trial was to be the foundation for the new repression.

These pages are being written six months later. Bobby Seale is awaiting trial in Connecticut, where he faces the electric chair. Fred Hampton has been murdered in his bed by police. We have been convicted—not for what we did in 1968 but for the total crime of a disrespectful identity. Our conviction in turn provoked the first interstate white riot. Attorney William Kunstler, sentenced to four years on contempt charges for defending us, is now himself charged with provoking riots. And the "disruptions" that occurred during our trial now seem mild in comparison with what is happening in courtrooms in Maryland, Connecticut, and New York City. Bill Kunstler now "represents" H. Rap Brown, whose activities the anti-riot law was supposed to curb. Rap is nowhere to be seen, and two of his comrades have been murdered in Bel Air, Maryland. The Weathermen are splitting from trial appearances stemming from their mini-riot in October, and several of their leading members have died, apparently while making bombs in New York. The New York Panther Twenty-one—denied their constitutional rights by prohibitive bail—are still refusing to show "respect" for their trial judge. The Connecticut trial of Bobby Seale and eight other Panthers may prove to be the most explosive in U.S. history. And a wave of bombings and bomb threats has spread across the country, with politicians issuing warnings about the threat of "urban guerrilla warfare."

Bobby Rush was right that day—no one knew what we were getting into. The Conspiracy trial was both a nightmare and an awakening. Now, weeks after its conclusion, we are still trying to comprehend it. It was something out of Kafka's imagination—six months of living in Judge Hoffman's neon oven; a trial that symbolized the beginning of full-scale political repression in the United States; a trial of the entire protest generation of the 1960s; a trial that began as a unique confrontation in American courts but was quickly surpassed in intensity by the very upsurge of new confrontations it helped to provoke.

From Protest
to Resistance

I

1968: Repression

The trial became a watershed experience for an entire generation of alienated white youth. It symbolized our passage over that line separating the respectable from the criminal. From now on, even middle-class white children would no longer be safe from the paranoid wrath of the older, entrenched generation. We had seen it coming at the Pentagon, at Columbia, and in the streets of Chicago, and finally at People's Park, where murderous bullets were unleashed against tender white skin. The trial brought all these isolated lessons into a single focus.

Future histories will locate the late sixties as the time when America's famous democratic pragmatism began hardening into an inflexible fascist core. To those of us living these times, however, it has come as something of a surprise. The New Leftists of the early sixties, and many of the black radicals as well, were preoccupied not with the danger of fascist repression but with that of liberal co-optation. We saw a power structure with such vast wealth and weaponry that it seemed beyond defeat. More than that, it seemed capable of preventing even the emergence of a real political challenge. Because of the generally high standard of living and the system's adaptability to social pressures, we seemed doomed to exist only as a marginal force. We accepted Mills and the early Marcuse as prophets of a new social order that had managed to stabilize all its major contradictions.

In focusing on the co-optive mechanisms of the society, we were recognizing something unique in America that traditional Marxism said little about. Yet time has proven how wrong we were to fasten on this aspect of the American system. The civil-rights movement was not co-opted but rebuffed and driven toward black power and then on to revolutionary demands. At every step the blacks met with increased official violence. Meanwhile, the war in Vietnam was not ended as a "mistake" (as both liberals and radicals had predicted) but instead was escalated into an all-out conflict stretching through three countries. In a less violent way, the student and youth movements of the early sixties were not absorbed (via the eighteen-year-old vote, legalization of drugs, establishment of student rights, etc.) but were blocked from securing even the smallest footholds of power.

For a time it was customary to believe that the officials who continued to reject our demands were either blind or stupid. We actually believed that we knew how to run their system more cleverly and effectively than they did. But the consistent intransigence of men in power caused a search for a more adequate explanation.

Perhaps the truth is that these men of power, and their vast empire, are not so powerful as we supposed them to be. From the early forties to the early sixties, the period in which the present younger generation was shaped, there was no doubt that the American Empire was the most powerful in the world. In a time of such international predominance, it was possible for our government to be relatively flexible and tolerant toward dissent at home. But with the growth of the black-liberation movement, the Cuban revolution, and the Vietnamese and Laotian revolutionary wars, a new era of confrontation was defined. The United States became the banking and military headquarters of counterrevolution throughout the world. As revolution spread, even reaching inside the United States itself, the costs to the American system soared sharply. The economic burden threatened our gold reserves and made any domestic welfare reforms impossible. The political and moral cost could be counted in the division of races and generations, resulting in the growth of a new American radicalism for the first time since the thirties. Faced with these threats, a choice between Empire and Democracy became necessary. It would be impossible to act as International Gendarme while permitting mass movements to threaten the power structure at home. The pursuit of imperialism created a necessity for repression, even fascism, to stabilize the home front.

But these are reflections after the fact. During the pivotal year of 1968 we were as unclear as anyone else about the whirlwind toward which we were plunging. In our experience of the sixties, the right to organize protest seemed protected, however weakly, by the courts. In fact, since the 1954 school-desegregation decisions, and especially in the early 1960s, the higher courts were used against local authorities to protect civil liberties. The struggle in Mississippi from 1960 to 1964 was primarily a battle to get the federal government to extend civil liberties—the right to organize—to a state that then seemed "backward." In that struggle the federal government and higher courts tended to support the right to protest.

When the Vietnam escalation began in 1965, the government still did not intervene against the growing dissent. The fact that opposition was allowed even in time of major—if undeclared—war seemed once again to confirm America's extreme flexibility. Jean-Paul Sartre refused to speak at teach-ins in the United States for fear that he would reinforce the myth that America was a democratic society. His fear, we would find, was vastly exaggerated, but at the time nearly everyone agreed that our protest would be contained, rather than repressed.

The same tolerance was evident on the cultural front. Despite widespread restrictions against the use of drugs, the courts were never really employed as an instrument for cracking down on the new youth culture. Even Julius

Hoffman ruled in the fifties that William Burroughs' *Naked Lunch* could be sent across state lines in the mail—while fifteen years later he was offended that its author would live out his fantasies in the streets of Chicago.

And so, in the beginning of 1968, we planned a protest at the Democratic Convention that we believed might be militant and chaotic, possibly even violent in some ways, but nevertheless legal and permissible. We could see the rise of repression in the smoldering ghettos, but we had given only minor attention to the proposal of Southern congressmen in the fall of 1967 to pass a new federal law against those who crossed state lines to cause "riots." It seemed like more of the legislation that Southerners always proposed and that federal authorities always rejected.

The first warning of real repression against ourselves came, paradoxically, from Stokely Carmichael, the target of the Southerners' anti-riot bill. I met him in January 1968 to discuss our projected demonstrations in Chicago. Stokely had just returned from an international trip in which he had had a chance to evaluate the conflict between U.S. imperialism and wars of liberation on three continents. Although the assassinations and major violence of 1968 had not yet occurred, he already sensed a new level of repressive violence ahead. He warned us to be careful in laying plans for Chicago because, he said, the Democrats would smash hippie heads if only to undercut the popularity of George Wallace.

The smell of trouble was unmistakable three months later with the murder of Martin Luther King. In the demonstrations of rage that followed the assassination, the Chicago police killed several blacks on the West Side. Then on April 15 Mayor Daley urged police to "shoot to kill" arsonists and "maim or cripple" looters in the event of future rebellions. Two weeks later, on April 27, a peaceful and traditional antiwar demonstration, viewed by all sides as a warm-up for Convention Week, was brutally attacked by the Chicago police. The Cook County sheriff also announced plans to deputize citizens from areas such as Cicero into a reserve "vigilante" force during Convention Week, adding that tunnels below the city might be opened as detention camps for persons arrested in August.

At the national level the trend toward repression was crystallized in the sudden passage of the anti-riot law as part of a "tribute" to Martin Luther King. The blaming of demonic outside agitators for social "unrest," a response that had been dismissed as raving and irresponsible when it came from Southern sheriffs in the early sixties, was now being endorsed as a national philosophy. The new legislation would allow the federal government—particularly the Justice Department, the FBI, and the Pentagon—to move into local crises on a coordinated basis. With the passage of this legislation the Southern Way of Life, generally regarded in 1960 as immoral and archaic, had become synonymous with the American Way of Life.

The new law was not aimed at preventing violence and disruption per se. It exempted, for example, all union organizing—activities that often involve interstate travelers who cause whole industries to be paralyzed. Nor was the law simply aimed at people involved in riots; for that purpose every state has its own anti-riot law. The legislation represented a new policy commitment at the national level, aimed, as the Congressional Record makes evident, at an entire decade of protest, at every movement of social significance from the early freedom rides in the South to the Pentagon demonstration of 1967. It was aimed at everyone, violent or nonviolent, whose experience in the sixties had led them to conclude that there were no effective "proper" channels for the redress of grievances in this society, and that it therefore was necessary to create new forms of protest and open new channels of social change.

From that point forward we knew we were organizing under new conditions, in the shadow of a law that could well be aimed at ourselves. The murder of Kennedy two months later seemed to underscore the fact that violence was in store for anyone—even those safely within the system—who wanted at least a modification of American policies. The consistent refusal of Democratic officials in Chicago to negotiate with us for permits also was a warning that a new line was coming down from somewhere. We sensed only that we were entering into a new and dangerous situation in which traditional methods of organizing protest were outlawed or obsolete. Our role in the unfolding drama was not made clear until August 26, the opening day of the Convention, when I was arrested and told that the FBI was preparing to "get us" for inciting to riot across state lines.

II

Convention Week

Whatever else Chicago 1968 was, it was not the "spontaneous police riot" described in the Walker Report. Certainly there were cases of individual policemen breaking orders and going berserk—throwing young women into Lincoln Park lagoon, shooting through the ceilings of the Chicago Art Museum. These were not isolated acts, however, but acts generated by official policies that deliberately created the major episodes of police violence in Chicago:

• Clearing Lincoln Park every night to enforce an absurd curfew, driving people into the streets, and covering Lincoln Park with gas.

• Marching with swinging clubs into a seated crowd in the Grant Park bandshell after someone pulled down the American flag on the afternoon of August 28.

• Smashing into a peaceful, chanting crowd later that night, that for a few minutes, was clogging the intersection in front of the Conrad Hilton.

Police claim, often with the concurrence of liberals, that they were "provoked" by obscenity, long hair, and occasional missiles hurled from the crowds. Police are supposed to be professionally trained to withstand provocation of all kinds. In any case, obscenity is nothing new to them; long hair was a normal sight at every Sunday music festival they patrolled that summer in Lincoln Park; and the missiles were invariably thrown after—not before—a police attack.

It is police strategy and tactics, not the rhetoric and appearance of agitators, that determine how an unorganized crowd will behave. We did not come to Chicago with the term "pig" in our vocabulary, and we did not imagine beforehand the slogan "The streets belong to the people." But those words made sense in the situation that was created by the police. By clearing the park, they drove people into the streets all night. By attacking peaceful assemblies, religious meetings, even the McCarthy headquarters in the Conrad Hilton, the police created a profoundly unifying experience for all the diverse people who gathered that week in Chicago.

Police always have a range of options for crowd control. At one extreme, they can grant permits for demonstrations and keep a minimum of police present, with reserves nearby. At the other extreme is the full denial of the constitutional right of assembly accompanied by military occupation. What makes the police choose the harder line is not the *military* threat presented by the demonstrators (which is usually nonexistent when compared to their own deterrent strength). The police take the harder line to make a *political* point, to frighten and intimidate.

This same pattern of police behavior was clear on a larger scale during the black uprisings of the previous year. In Newark, for example, the blacks took over and looted a small section of the central ghetto on the first night, after the police had provoked an incident by beating up a black cabdriver in full sight of several citizens. On the second night the looting expanded (although it remained within the central ghetto) when the police started shooting. The police rationale was that arson and sniping, as well as looting, were taking place. The truth was that there was virtually no arson or sniping. The police were killing people for breaking into stores and for the deeper crime of expressing the desire for self-determi-

nation. In response to police calls, the National Guard occupied the community. They could have encircled the ghetto
"protecting downtown business and nearby white communities" and retained a minimum presence, or they could have
placed a black police presence in the ghetto. Most of the
looting was completed by the time the National Guard came
(it can be done faster than a National Guard can be mobilized), and the people were hardly going to burn down their
own homes or snipe at each other. But the troops were sent in
flying squads, patrolling the streets, constantly provoking
people with guns and bayonets, and forcing them back into
their homes. There was no pure military reason for this. The
central purpose had to be political—to intimidate and punish
the blacks for their rebellion, to reassert authority forcefully,
and to stampede white voters to the right with frightening racial propaganda. In other words, the police response was not
the only policy alternative available to city and state officials.
It was an alternative intentionally chosen by men bent on ex-
aggerating the immediate danger of a crisis because of the
ultimate threat that the crisis represented. Chicago was pro-
grammed, too. We were to be the new-style niggers.

But if Chicago was planned, why and by whom, and who
benefited? Searching for an answer is not simply an intellectual exercise, since the answer might shed light on both why
and how America has headed down the road to repression.
Taken together, the Chicago confrontations of 1968 in the
streets and of 1969 in the courtroom place in sharp focus the
relationship between rebellion and repression.

In his introduction to Jerry Rubin's book *Do It,* Eldridge
Cleaver gives one coherent explanation of what happened in
Chicago. Rejecting the notion that the police "flipped out,"
Eldridge argues that a right-wing conspiracy to elect Nixon
set up the confrontation to discredit the Democrats and
stampede a frightened public toward more conservative electoral choices. He warns that the tactic of the right wing is al-

ways to inflate the threat of the left in order to create anxieties among people that can be exploded by would-be fascists.

Dick Gregory takes an even more conspiratorial view of what occurred in Chicago, a view to which he testified at the trial. According to Gregory, the CIA was trying to "overthrow the country," was implicated in the deaths of Dr. King and both Kennedys, and was planning the assassination of black leaders, including himself, in Chicago as a pretext for using the pre-positioned U.S. troops against the ghetto.

Both of these speculations suppose a single-minded government conspiracy against dissent without focusing on the bipartisan political coalition that wanted repression in 1968. Eldridge's analysis does not explain why Mayor Daley and the Democrats would want to throw an election to the Republicans. It ignores the fact that it was the Democratic Party that planned the police violence. No doubt local pride and chauvinism influenced Daley, but as a professional politician he probably believed that the Democrats could win only by outdoing Nixon and Wallace at law and order. Instead of throwing the election to Nixon, Daley probably wanted to upstage him.

The problem with Gregory's view is that it involves controversial claims that are not necessary prerequisites for people who agree with his general conclusion. Certainly Dr. King and perhaps both Kennedys were killed by right-wing elements with official connections. A real investigation into the killings would yield explosive results. But regardless of who those specific assassins turn out to be, it is the general attitude of the American right that it is necessary to use violence and repression to destroy not only hard-core radicalism but the liberalism that fosters it as well.

The assassination of popular leaders is only one tactic among many for achieving this result. In 1968 the right wanted to stop not only the freaks in the street but the liberal Democratic senators who urged permits for the demonstrations; and in 1969, in the courtroom, it wanted to stop not only the defendants but their lawyers as well.

Any explanation of Chicago must begin with the fact that a violent and repressive element of the Democratic Party took power over domestic affairs, as it already had over foreign policy. The Chicago Convention marked the triumph for this element in a dispute that divided the party at the highest level in its attitude toward protest.

Some of this murky history came out at the trial in the testimony of Justice Department officials and in interviews with Ramsey Clark, who was not allowed to testify. A deep split apparently developed in 1968 between Clark and Mayor Daley over Chicago's handling of the black rebellion. Clark termed Daley's shoot-to-kill order "unlawful and unthinkable," and no real communication took place between the two men after that. In July Clark dispatched the head of his Community Relations Service, Roger Wilkins, and a law-enforcement specialist, Wesley Pomeroy, in an effort to get permit negotiations under way in Chicago. According to Clark, the Justice Department officials found Rennie Davis responsive but got nowhere with Daley.

During this same period, Clark evidently was becoming completely isolated within higher government circles. He rejected FBI evaluations of dissenters, including several members of the Conspiracy, and refused to warrant wiretapping of our phones. His handling of the Poor People's Campaign in the spring of 1968 drew the wrath of other federal officials. During that campaign, although Clark's mediators kept violence to a minimum around Resurrection City (an effort after which Chicago officials could have modeled their efforts), the Attorney General was blamed for the general spectacle and for the embarrassing protests held at various government agencies.

About one week before the Convention, a critical meeting was held in the Oval Room of the White House. Present at this meeting were Lyndon Johnson, members of the White

House staff, Defense Department officials, and Clark. Daley and Police Superintendent James Conlisk had called for the pre-positioning of 5000 federal troops near Chicago; Conlisk cited articles in the *Berkeley Barb* as part of his justification. Only the Attorney General advised against moving the troops, claiming it would have "disastrous policy implications" by creating a climate of expectation that the troops would be used.

This political conflict summarized the general crisis of the 1960s, in which those liberals who had worked with protest to improve the system (Clark, Kennedy, McCarthy) became increasingly divided from those conservatives who would prevent the spread of protest by any means necessary (Johnson, Nixon).

The Chicago Convention, as Miami before, represented the final rout of liberal politics and the political establishment's adoption of the repressive outlook that had been integral to U.S. foreign policy for the last two decades but that on the domestic scene had been associated only with the conservative and extreme right. Those liberal politicians who did not adjust their attitudes to the times found themselves isolated and impotent; the more supple and politically ambitious, like Humphrey, leapt into the new and warm embrace of comrades like Lester Maddox. It was an unexpected but appropriate irony that Nixon and Humphrey, the conservative and liberal architects of the bipartisan cold-war strategy of the late forties, became in 1968 the leaders of a bipartisan coalition to bring the cold war home.

III

The New Party Line

The change in national policy was reflected in decisions immediately after the convention. Ramsey Clark called Tom Foran, the U.S. Attorney in Chicago, who would eventually become our prosecutor. Clark ordered an investigation of possible infractions of civil-rights codes (police brutality), especially the clubbings at Michigan and Balbo on August 28 (which caused Wes Pomeroy to tell the Attorney General by telephone, "I'm ashamed to be a policeman") and the invasion of the McCarthy headquarters in the Conrad Hilton late on the night of August 29. Most important, he suggested that no grand jury be convened to investigate us or any other alleged provocateurs, but that the investigation be conducted by the U.S. Attorneys. One week later, Federal Judge William Campbell not only convened the grand jury but ordered that no one from the Justice Department participate except persons from Foran's office. Though this order was later vacated, it symbolized the determination to get federal conspiracy indictments even over the will of the incumbent Attorney General. In the wake of our trial, this was further confirmed by men who ought to know: Representative Cramer, the Florida congressman who had helped to author the anti-riot law, charged that Ramsey Clark had been "dragging his feet" while in office, and Tom Foran acknowledged in the press that it was John Mitchell who finally authorized the prosecution of the Conspiracy.

All that remained was for the Democrats to lose the election. They never recovered from the Convention. Televised police clubs fell on every liberal in the country, and the grass-roots base of the Democratic Party's campaign fell away. Nixon, a loser if there ever was one, entered office as an illegitimate President, without a shred of authorization from the blacks and the young. Despite all his talk about "bringing us together," he was destined to be a minority President, or at best a President of half the people. Despite talk of a new Nixon, this was only an improved Madison Avenue version of the same man who had pursued Alger Hiss and other "un-Americans," who had advocated that American troops be sent to Vietnam in 1954, and who has acted, since the 1950s, as if black people did not exist as a constituency in the United States. Here was a man installed in our highest office, but already obsolete, a Horatio Alger striving in the corporate America of the organization man. His only mandate from the people who provided the bulk of his support was to embark on a program of trying to hold back the future.

The future was being born in Chicago, but as Carl Oglesby declared, there were undertakers in the delivery room. Nixon's undertakers were positioned in the Justice Department and the judiciary: Attorney General John Mitchell, a conservative corporation lawyer, an old friend of Nixon's, and a party politician; Deputy Attorney General Richard Kleindienst, the former Goldwaterite engaged in a holy war with communism who once said, "If people demonstrate in a manner to interfere with others, they should be rounded up and put in a detention camp"; civil-rights division head Jerris Leonard, a member of racially exclusive clubs in Milwaukee and a former Wisconsin bond commissioner who funded $200,000 in fees to Mitchell; in the criminal division, Will Wilson, a reactionary Texas politician, also on record as calling for detention camps; and Chief Justice of the U. S. Supreme Court Warren Burger, a "strict constructionist" who supported McCarthyism in the 1950s. For Associate

Justice of the Supreme Court Nixon proposed Clement Haynsworth and then G. Harold Carswell, both far-right Southern racists. And if these men needed a demagogic spokesman to make them appear respectable, they found one in Spiro T. Agnew.

These new men, who have taken over the Justice Department and the high courts, have a simple ideology and program. They believe that twenty-five years of permissive liberalism has produced demands for "too much too soon" by blacks and has nurtured a younger generation with no respect for authority. They see the foundations of civilization— the nuclear family and free enterprise—disintegrating. They see a disciplined world communist movement steadily developing the ability to defeat the United States, not primarily through force of arms but through the subversion of Western moral authority.

Their program is to apply the brakes to all liberalizing tendencies and to use stern punishment against the radicals. Their "strict constructionism" is a euphemism for "legally" overthrowing the government as it has operated since 1954.

Racism is the immediate institution that they seek to prolong, and they can do so more aggressively than the Democrats ever dreamed of. The Republicans do not have a black constituency like the Democrats; in fact, they need to win over a white racist constituency from George Wallace. The two prongs of their racial repression are clear: first, to cut back all forms of desegregation and federal programs for blacks; and second, to organize a full-scale safari against the Black Panthers and other black revolutionaries.

At the same time, they programmatically seek to weaken dissent in general. They are now attacking, at all levels, the right to organize. First, the mere existence of the new Justice Department gives the green light for local prosecutors and police to crack down. Second, government agencies at all levels are being purged of honest officials sympathetic or tolerant toward protest. Third, special task forces have been established in the Justice Department to go after the Panthers and other groups.

We always believed that one of the covert reasons for our prosecution was that, in the minds of Justice Department officials, six of the Conspiracy defendants were identified as ringleaders not only of the events at Chicago but of much of the turmoil of the 1960s: the confrontations in Berkeley, at Columbia, at the Pentagon; the growth of the hippie culture; and the internationalizing of the anti-war movement. Typical of government reasoning, for instance, was a Justice Department memo tracing the beginning of the anti-war resistance to a meeting between David Dellinger and Ho Chi Minh in 1967.

But going after the Chicago Conspiracy indictments was only one of the more publicized parts of the overall Justice Department program, and using the absurd anti-riot law was one of many steps taken to tighten the restrictions on public expression in the United States. Other, more permanent forms of repression have been implemented with little or no public attention.

Thus, for example, the expansion of wiretapping is a clear case of the government going beyond constitutional limitations to establish new controls. Previously, it was necessary for federal officials to obtain wiretap authorization through a court hearing. In our trial the government first asserted the right to wiretap with only the authorization of the President when "national security" is involved. This is only one example of the government introducing foreign-policy espionage tactics against American citizens. It is less well known, for instance, that the Pentagon has a domestic counterinsurgency section, and that the U.S. Army keeps files on domestic "subversives." (Two of the undercover agents testifying against us in the trial, for example, were from Army and Navy intelligence.)

These measures and others are designed to enforce a new

limited doctrine of "free speech." Traditional law protects speech—*any speech*—unless it constitutes some kind of "clear and present danger" to the social order. This means that one has the right to advocate overthrowing the government or disrupting the Democratic Convention as long as the words are not immediately carried out by the listening audience. It means that one has the freedom to be ineffective. But under the new doctrine the speeches we gave on civil disobedience months before the Convention, for example, were used as part of the evidence showing that our "state of mind" was criminal. Whatever we said in peaceful assemblies, in churches, or to the news media was eventually collected as part of the evidence proving our guilt for what finally happened in Chicago.

The dangers of this doctrine are obvious. First, police agents habitually misinterpret radical language and intent; and second, under the doctrine a spokesman becomes responsible for any violence or illegal activity occurring at a demonstration he plans or encourages. If it can be proven that you have a defiant and rebellious "state of mind," you can be indicted even if your only concrete act is bringing people on a bus to Chicago.

This state of mind, according to the Justice Department, is characteristic of a new breed of subversive, the "ideological criminal." The crime of this sort of person is quite simply disbelief in American institutions. The ideological criminal is not necessarily a knowing instrument of a worldwide or even a communist conspiracy. Those were the criminal categories of the 1950s. The ideological criminal is known not by his affiliation with organizations but by his *disaffiliation* from the conventional methods of pursuing change. Anyone distrusting the orthodox channels of change is considered a social misfit or a nihilist.

When the government assumes this right to jail people because of their consciousness, we are already living in 1984.

A Generation
on Trial

IV

Our Identity on Trial

Our kids don't understand that we don't mean anything when we use the word "nigger" . . . they just look at us like we were a bunch of dinosaurs . . . we've lost our kids to the freaking fag revolution.
—PROSECUTING ATTORNEY THOMAS FORAN
in a speech after the trial

Our crime was our identity. Even the sympathetic press misunderstood, billing our case as one of "dissent on trial." So did Bill Kunstler in the beginning, when he spoke of repression of "the spectrum of dissent" and implied that we differed from other Americans only in our political opinions. Although there was a certain amount of obvious truth in this claim, it always seemed superficial to us.

The vague nature of the government's case made us feel we were on trial for something deeper and unspoken. The charges against us made no sense. We spent endless hours trying to comprehend what the case was all about.

Against our common sense the government kept insisting that the trial was not "political," not about the Vietnam war, not about the Black Panther Party, but simply the prosecution of a criminal indictment. It was, for the government, a question of whether we had conspired to cross state lines with the intention of organizing, promoting, or encouraging a riot. To prove its case it relied on evidence from Chicago policemen, undercover and FBI agents, Army and Navy personnel, two *Chicago Tribune* reporters, and only two civilians with no apparent police connections.

Despite its claims, however, the government presented little evidence of "conspiracy." In fact, government attorney Richard Schultz acknowledged that we never all met together, not even once. Bobby Seale never met any of us until coming to Chicago, and then he met only Jerry Rubin. Evidence of conspiracy in a criminal trial, however, defies the everyday imagination. The government argued that it was necessary only that we "shared a common design." But even if we did, why only the eight of us? Why not several of the other "unindicted co-conspirators" who seemed, from the government's evidence, to have done more in Chicago than had several of us? Why not Dick Gregory, who had announced that the Convention would take place "over his dead body" and then, after withdrawing from the planning, returned to lead a march at which more arrests were made than at any other time during Convention Week? Why not Norman Mailer, whom we invited to speak and who told an angry assembly that we were "at the beginning of a war and the march immediately afterwards would be one battle in that war"?

We became the Conspiracy not because we did anything together in 1968 but simply because we were indicted together. We became closely knit because of the trial, and perhaps the government was relying on this very process for its proof. By intertwining our names through the testimony (as if the words and evidence reflected the reality of 1968) while we sat together at the defense table for five months, it might begin to appear to a jury that we always had been an interconnected unit. But evidently it never convinced the jury, and it certainly made us feel strange, like survivors of a shipwreck getting to know one another because we shared the same raft.

As for concrete evidence of lawbreaking activity, the government puzzled us further by introducing almost nothing.

David Dellinger, Rennie Davis, Abbie Hoffman: nothing at all. Tom Hayden: one arrest for letting the air out of a police tire, another for spitting at an arresting officer and, in addition, adopting disguises to avoid the police. Jerry Rubin: charged with throwing a sweater at his "tail" and for being in the presence of others who threw a bottle of paint at a police car (and missed). At first we supposed that John Froines and Lee Weiner had been indicted because of heavy evidence of hard acts, but again we had exaggerated the government's case. Froines and Weiner supposedly participated in a discussion, the day after the presidential nomination, in which plans were made to firebomb an underground garage in the Loop. The bombing, according to the government, would "divert" the police from Loop demonstrations. Strangely, however, according to the government's own witnesses, the Mobilization had already ended its Convention protests that very morning, and the only demonstrations Weiner was going to "aid" were led by Dick Gregory and Convention delegates, who were not indicted. Stranger yet, the indictments charged Weiner with "teaching and demonstrating the use of incendiary devices," but no evidence was given during the entire trial of any such instruction on his part. Strangest of all, the bombing never took place and none of the alleged bombers or any of their materials appeared in city, state, or federal courts.

Froines was further indicted for conspiring to stinkbomb the Convention hotels. The truth is that several women, whom some of us knew, carried out some stinkbombing and were arrested, convicted, fined, and placed on probation. None of them was indicted on federal charges (probably because a male-supremacist government does not believe that women are capable of action independent of the knowledge and control of men). John was indicted because he had purchased butyric acid for someone (not any of the women we knew of); and because of his chemistry credentials, the government hoped to make him appear to the jury to be a diabolical scientist. The major stinkbombing evidence consisted only of a 3 A.M. "attack" (drops of the fluid were found on tissues) in the Charade-a-go-go, a nightclub frequented by delegates after their Convention responsibilities were discharged. So the jury didn't buy the bomb plot. John and Lee, the only two conspirators charged with concrete lawbreaking activity, were acquitted.

Since the evidence of conspiracy and concrete illegal activity was so weak, the thrust of the government's attack had to be carried out against our "state of mind." As we sat through the months of testimony about our consciousness, we began to realize that the charges against us were really just as *total* as the changes we wanted to make in American society. On the surface there was evidence of conversations, speeches, and plots hatched in the presence of undercover government agents. Many of these were wholly fabricated; others were twisted accounts. The accurate ones—those recorded on tape—were never difficult to justify legally. But just below the surface of the testimony there was always the implication that we were dangerous and alien to the America of the jury.

It was not dissent that was on trial, the government maintained. It had no quarrel with those who "oppose" the Vietnam war and racism or those who "favor" new kinds of relationships between people. The government in fact claimed it did not mind if "legitimate" people did many of the very things we were charged with doing. The prosecutor practically bowed and scraped before Representative Julian Bond, for instance, who was not allowed to testify that he too thought of calling the Chicago policemen "pigs"; before Congressman John Conyers, who was arrested on the Convention floor; and before Ralph Abernathy, who used the word "pig" for the first time in Chicago and described himself as a Yippie. Dr. Spock was treated by Judge Hoffman as a respected baby doctor, and Dick Gregory became his favorite comedian. The government had nothing against protest; it was opposed only to the evil that we allegedly injected into legitimate protest activities.

Our crime was that we were beginning to live a new and contagious life style without official authorization. We were tried for being out of control.

First of all, we were internationalists. Not only did we oppose racism; we aligned ourselves with people like Bobby Seale. Not only were we against the war in Vietnam; we aligned ourselves with the Vietnamese people. These were not simply "positions" we took; they were more like the natural reflexes of new human beings trying to be relevant to the world as it is. *The world we see is one in which a decadent and super-rich American empire, with its principles of racial superiority, private property, and armed might, is falling apart. We want to join with the new humanity, not support a dying empire.* We make our judgments according to universal and international principles of social justice, not according to a "national interest." This internationalism leads us to identify with peoples whom the U.S. government defines as enemies. It led Rennie, Dave, and me twice to Vietnam; it led us all to close solidarity with the black-liberation struggle; it led us to place Che's portrait on our defense table on the anniversary of his assassination and to ask Bill Kunstler to speak of Che's spirit in his summation to the jury.

Our most "disruptive" behavior in court, besides attacks on the judge's vanity, seemed to be our support for Bobby. And although we felt we hadn't done enough by merely protesting in court, the judge still saw us as a disgrace to the white race. At the end of the trial he was still asking us if we believed, with Bobby, that George Washington (whose portrait was on the wall) was a slavemaster. At one point Hoffman even threatened to revoke our bail unless we broke our solidarity with Bobby's position. He gave us lunchtime to think it over, but then he mysteriously backed down.

Another example of the internationalism that upset the court was our placing of a National Liberation Front flag on the defense table alongside the American flag during the October Moratorium. For ourselves, it was an affirmation of the belief that our people are not at war with the people of Vietnam. The judge did not comment on the propriety of Dave's trying to read the names of the war dead that day, but he ranted and never forgot about "the flag of an enemy country" appearing in his courtroom. The U.S. marshals not only ripped off this NLF flag; a few minutes later they felt compelled to return for the American one, as if it were disgraced by the likes of us.

It turned out that the presence of an NLF flag was always "proof" in the government's eyes that our marches in Chicago in 1968 were illegitimate. At first we were puzzled as to why the government would introduce as part of its evidence films that showed rather orderly demonstrations. The reason, we finally realized, was the close-up color photographs of NLF flags in the film. In the cross-examinations of Linda Morse and Rennie, the prosecutors were visibly excited by establishing that we favored a revolution by a liberation movement "just like the Vietcong." Foran even thought it was incriminating to get Rennie to admit he believed that the Vietcong were "like some of the early American patriots," and that America was now an "imperial country just like England in the eighteenth century."

Our underlying crime, the evidence of which was revealed every day in the courtroom, was that we were beginning to live a new life style beyond that of capitalist America. Our defense table was a "liberated zone" right in front of the jury's eyes. The room itself was a sterile horror, shaped like a box, the doors smoothly tucked into the walls, neon lighting casting illumination without shadow, as if people did not exist. Paintings of British and American historical figures hung above the bench and just below the Great Seal of the United States. It was a heavy decorum. As many as twenty federal marshals kept "order," instructing spectators that they could not laugh, fall asleep, read, or go to the bathroom without forfeiting their seats. The government's table, nearer the jury, was impeccably clean, the four-member team invariably dressed in gray flannel or, in the case of Foran, sporty gabardine suits. The jury, dressed neatly as well, obeyed their orders to say good morning to the judge but otherwise remained quiet and expressionless throughout the proceedings. The judge, his old man's head attached to his floating robe like a bizarre puppet, called for respect in his gravely, sonorous, vain tone. And there we were, supposedly the victims but somehow the center of everything: our hair growing longer with each passing month; our clothes ranging from hip to shabby; joking, whispering seriously, passing notes, reading newspapers, and ignoring testimony and the rules of the judge; occasionally looking for friendly jurors' faces but eventually giving up and just being ourselves. This behavior was the ultimate defiance of a court system that demands the repression of people into well-behaved clients, advocates, and jurors.

The conflict of life styles emerged not simply around our internationalism but perhaps even more around "cultural" and "psychological" issues. For instance, music. When Arlo Guthrie, Judy Collins, Phil Ochs, Country Joe, Pete Seeger, and others tried to sing for the jury, they were admonished that "this is a criminal trial, not a theater." No one, including the press, understood what was going on. From the judge to the most liberal journalist there was a consensus that we were engaged in a put-on, a further "mockery of the court." They seemed incapable of coming to terms with the challenge on any deeper level. The court's concession was that the words to the songs, but not the singing of them, were admissible. But this was a compromise that missed the entire point. The words of "Alice's Restaurant," "We Ain't A-Marchin' Any More," "Vietnam Rag," "Where Have All the Flowers Gone," and "Wasn't That a Time" may be moving even when they are spoken, but the words gained their meaning in this generation because they were *sung*. To understand their meaning would be to understand the meaning of music to the new consciousness. From the beginning of rock and roll, there has grown up a generation of young whites with a new, less repressed attitude toward sex and pleasure, and music has been the medium of their liberation. When Phil Ochs sang "We Ain't A-Marchin' Any More" in Chicago during the Convention, it provoked a pandemonium of emotion, of collective power, that spoken words could not have done. Singing in that courtroom would have jarred its decorum, but that very decorum was oppressing our identity and our legal defense.

Or, for instance, sex. Government attorney Tom Foran's post-trial statement about the "freaking fag revolution" merely confirmed what we could see throughout. Foran represented imperialist, aggressive man, while we, for all our male chauvinist tendencies, represented a gentler, less aggressive type of human being. Schultz kept returning to the phrase "public fornication" as though the words themselves were a crime, since the government introduced no testimony to show that Yippies had acted on this threat (except once in a tree, according to an undercover agent). Allen Ginsberg was cross-examined as to whether he had "intimate" relationships with Abbie and Jerry. Physical affection between the defendants and their friends and witnesses was always noted by either the judge or the prosecution for the record. The scene of Bill Kunstler hugging Ralph Abernathy was particularly offensive to the judge, who declared that he had never seen so much "physical affection in my courtroom."

The conflict of identity on this level was sharpest during Ginsberg's testimony. Most commentators have reduced that episode to Allen's "chanting." The fact is that Allen was allowed to do very little chanting, and even this was as misunderstood as the singing of other witnesses. Actually, Allen was one of the few witnesses to state directly the terms of the conflict that is emerging. He testified that he had favored a Festival of Life in Chicago because

. . . the planet Earth was endangered by violence, overpopulation, pollution, ecological destruction, brought on by our own greed . . . that it was a planetary crisis that had not been recognized by any government in the world . . . the more selfish older politicians were not thinking in terms of what their children would need in future generations . . . and were continuing to threaten the planet with violence, with war, with mass murder, with germ warfare. . . .

During this part of his testimony, Allen explained and tried to perform the chant that became an "outburst" to the press. The "Hare Krishna" is an Indian *mantra* chanted to the preserver god, Vishnu, whenever the planet and human life are threatened. Allen later performed the "Om" chant, which is used to prevent crowd panic by re-establishing inner calm in individuals. Although the government wanted its witnesses to recite *inflammatory* chants (the kind that agitators in the movies are supposed to use), it opposed Allen's introducing and explaining *these* chants.

The conflict came out into the open during Foran's cross-examination. Instead of questioning Allen about anything he had testified to—such as pre-Convention planning by the Yippies and permit negotiations—Foran asked him to recite and explain three sexual poems apparently selected by the Justice Department agent at the table, a young, bespectacled, high-voiced, short-haired, blue-eyed young man named Cubbage. The first was about a wet dream, the second about a self-conscious young man at a party who discovers that he is eating an asshole sandwich, the third about a fantasy of sleeping between a man and a woman on their wedding night. At Foran's request Allen recited each one calmly and seriously and then tried to answer the prosecutor's sarcastic query about their religious significance. About the third

poem Allen stated that he had borrowed an image from Walt
Whitman, one of his "spiritual teachers," then explained:.

As part of our nature we have many loves, many of which are suppressed, many of which are denied, many of which we deny to ourselves. He [Whitman] said that the reclaiming of those loves and
the becoming aware of those loves was the only way that this.na-
tion could save itself and become a democratic and spiritual repub-
lic. He said that unless there was an infusion of feeling, of tender-
ness, of fearlessness, of spirituality, of natural sexuality, of natural
delight in each other's bodies, into the hardened, materialistic, cynical, life-denying, clearly competitive, afraid, scared, armored
bodies, there would be no chance for spiritual democracy to take
root in America. . . .

But the entire trial was structured to crush this vision of
Walt Whitman and Allen Ginsberg. The Federal Building itself was once described by the Chicago Art Institute as a
building in which "the commitment to order everywhere
present is translated into an authoritarian and heroic presence." And the appointed representatives of "the people" in
the courtroom itself—the jury—had received instructions
from the judge exactly opposite to the exhortations of Whitman and Ginsberg. Our jury was living not in a democracy
rooted in a communal and fraternal feeling but in a 1984
Palmer House way of life, totally dependent on government
marshals, a life of complete separation from their families
and fellow citizens. Above all, they were forbidden any
human contact—even questioning—with us, the people
whom they were to judge. This process of emotional denial
supposedly leads to "rationality," but it is precisely what
creates "hardened, materialistic, cynical, life-denying, clearly
competitive, afraid, scared, armored bodies."

On redirect examination, we asked Allen to recite "Howl."
We were not attempting to introduce "evidence" at this
point. Rather, if Foran wanted poetry, then we wanted to
hear the original poetic outcry of our times, an outcry which

begins "I saw the best minds of my generation destroyed by madness, starving, hysterical, naked . . ." and ends "They saw it all/the wild eyes/the holy yells/they bade farewell/they jumped off the roof to solitude/waving/carrying flowers/down to the river/into the street."

When Allen left the stand we were in tears. Court recessed a few minutes later, and Foran stared at Allen and said, "Damn fag."

A third example of the cultural conflict revolved around language. The government's case was a massive structure of obscene and provocative language attributed to us by police informers, language that the jury was supposed to imagine coming from our mouths as they stared at us across the courtroom. Some of the language was pure invention; most of it was a twisting of words that had once been used by us. Through the testimony over language, we came to the essence of the supposed "communication gap" between the generations.

The language of the Establishment is mutilated by hypocrisy. When "love" is used in advertising, "peace" in foreign policy, "freedom" in private enterprise, then these words have been stolen from their humanist origins, and new words become vital for the identity of people seeking to remake themselves and society. Negroes become "blacks," blacks become "Panthers," the oppressors become "pigs." Often the only words with emotional content are those that cannot be spoken or published in the "legitimate" world: fuck, motherfucker, shit and other "obscenities." New words are needed to express feelings: right on, cool, outta sight, freaky. New language becomes a weapon of the Movement because it is mysterious, threatening to conventional power: "We're gonna off the pig"; "We're gonna freak the delegates."

Clearly, some rhetoric of the left is wooden, inflated, irrelevant; crippling to the mind and an obstacle to communication. If we were interested in mild improvements to the system, perhaps we would use the prevailing language of the system. But one of the first tasks of those creating a new society is that of creating a new and distinct identity. This identity cannot be fully conscious at first, but as a movement grows, through years or generations, it contains its own body of experience, its styles and habits, and a common language becomes part of the new identity. The old language is depleted. In order to dream, to invoke anger or love, new language becomes necessary. Music and dance are forms of communication partly because they are directly expressive of feelings for which there is as yet no language.

(Part of the emphasis on "obscenity" was of course created through deliberate courtroom deceit by police witnesses who acted "ashamed" to repeat our words in the presence of the jury. But the deceit may have reflected a reality. Many policemen are vulgar with prostitutes, black prisoners, and fellow officers but "pure" toward their families, priests, and judges. One Chicago psychiatrist told us of several cases in which police wives filed for divorce because their husbands would not even make love with them. Policemen seem to regard women as either virgins or whores. This split life reflects a fear of "permissiveness" that is very much present when the police smash heads. They do it with the terrified excitement of children squashing bugs.)

Filtered through the mind of the police agent, language becomes criminal. The agent is looking for evidence; in fact, he has a vested interest in discovering evidence and begins with the assumption of guilt. Any reference to violence or blood, by an automatic mechanism in the police mind, means an offensive attack on constituted authorities. Our language thus becomes evidence of our criminality because it shows us to be outside the system. Perhaps our language would be acceptable if it were divorced from practice. Obscenity has always been allowed as part of free speech; it is the fact that our language is part of our action that is criminal. A jury of our peers would truly have been necessary for our language to have been judged, or even understood. Or at the very least, our middle-aged jury should have heard the expert testimony of someone who could partly bridge the communication gap.

Example: In July 1968 I gave a speech about the Vietnam war, most of which was an analysis of how the bombing halt and the peace talks were designed to undercut the anti-war movement. Toward the end I said that we in this country might have to shed our blood, just as the Vietnamese have shed theirs, if we were really serious about identifying with their suffering. I said further that the United States was violating its own laws in order to carry on the war and that it would be necessary for the protest movement to disregard the conventional rules of the game if it wanted to be effective. The FBI informer present at that meeting was from suburban New Jersey and was paid ten dollars plus expenses for attending meetings. He originally became an informer, he testified, at the request of a neighbor, an FBI agent, while they were chatting at a little league ballfield. Through the ears of this agent, my speech was "the most inflammatory speech I've ever heard in my life." He testified (sincerely, I'm sure) that I had called for "shedding blood" and "breaking rules" in Chicago.

Example: Police agent Tobin was following Rennie Davis on August 27, the first time the Chicago demonstrators stayed all night in front of the Conrad Hilton. At that time, Rennie had an impromptu sidewalk meeting with the deputy police superintendent, during which they agreed that people would be allowed in the park after the 11 P.M. curfew. Tobin testified that Rennie made a defiant speech fifteen minutes after their meeting to the effect that "the park is ours, stay in the park." Unfortunately for officer Tobin, his own grand-jury testimony had Rennie saying, "We *have* the park." The slightest change in the words had completely altered their substance.

Example: The government thought it highly incriminating when Norman Mailer testified that Jerry Rubin told him the presence of thousands of young longhairs in Chicago would "intimidate the Establishment." On cross-examination Mailer retracted the word "intimidate," declaring that it was impossible to recall words exactly; that Jerry probably wouldn't use a word like that—he would say something like "freak out." Mailer admitted that "intimidate" was more a word to his own liking because he had a bullying personality. "Words are nothing if not their nuance," he told the judge.

Len Weinglass stated the issue perfectly in his summation by quoting a passage from Matthew:

> Think not that I am come to send peace on earth
> I came not to send peace, but a sword
> For I am come to set man against his father
> And the daughter against her mother
> And a man's foes shall be they of his own household

As Len pointed out, a Chicago-style undercover agent listening to this biblical declaration probably would be left with the impression that Matthew had advocated the use of a sword against fathers and mothers. In fact, Christ's very existence—the idea he embodied—was sufficient to provoke the Establishment into violent overreaction.

Finally, the conflict of identities always involved the racism of the court toward Bobby. This showdown contained all the same elements—internationalism, culture, sex, language—but in a special framework that Eldridge described in *Soul on Ice*. The judge was the classic Omnipotent Administrator and Bobby his Supermasculine Menial. The sex and violence of the Menial are feared (Foran said Bobby was the only defendant who definitely "wasn't a fag"!). But even more threatening is any attempt by the Menial to assert his mind, to achieve power over his own life. The more the Menial asserts his ideas, Eldridge says, "the more emphatically will they be rejected and scorned by society, and treated as upstart invasions of the realm of the Omnipotent Administrator. . . . The struggle of his life is for the emancipation of his mind, to achieve recognition for the products of his mind, and official recognition of the fact that he has a mind."

There is no better way to explain why Hoffman continually and emphatically refused to let Bobby represent himself. "The complexity of the case makes self-representation inappropriate," the Administrator intoned.

V

A Note to Liberals

Since we were on trial for our identity and not merely for our words or deeds, the traditional notions of free speech and free assembly did not really apply to our case.

The rights guaranteed by the First Amendment are those of peaceful assembly, petitioning, and worship. These are the rights of the people in a pure democratic state. In such a system the people can make their needs known to officials and, if those needs are not met, replace their officials through elections. In this mythical rational system, the people supposedly form opinions freely, with the certainty that these opinions will be influential.

But when the democratic system is less than pure, when in fact it is corrupt, then First Amendment rights are ineffective and citizens have to return to the *origins* of the First Amendment and rediscover their own sovereignty. The root concept of the American Revolution was and still is: power to the people.

When authority becomes despotic, citizens have an absolute right to resistance. It was exactly this situation that faced the original American rebels, and it is exactly this situation that faces dissenters today. We are in a condition in which the First Amendment freedoms do not work effectively. Citizens have the right to speak, assemble, and protest freely until their actions begin to have a subversive effect on unresponsive authorities. It can be expressed as an axiom: at the point at which protest becomes effective, the state becomes repressive. Constitutional rights become primarily rhetorical. They are not extended to those who might use them to make basic structural change, to those who represent the beginning of a new society.

We faced arbitrary official power in the streets and in the courtrooms of Chicago. The officials naturally operated under the cover of "law," but what they meant by law was best expressed in *Catch-22:* "They can do anything they want to you as long as you can't stop them from doing it." The law they represented is always subservient to power. Abbie communicated this reality perfectly when he wore a black judicial robe to court with a blue Chicago police shirt underneath it.

Where this issue arose most sharply in 1968 was in our attempt to obtain permits for marching, rallying, and sleeping in the parks. Nothing should be more routine under the First Amendment that the issuing of permits. This is a normal city function conducted under vague municipal statutes that are rarely tested in the courts. Permits are supposed to be used to arrange and facilitate the expression of citizens' views, and city officials are supposed to limit such requests only to protect public safety, transportation, and so forth. Permits are not denied on holidays like St. Patrick's Day, when the major arteries of Chicago are swollen with marchers and the Chicago River is stained green, or during Shriners' conventions, when the parades occasionally become disorderly, with some of the participants known to urinate in the streets.

Our case demonstrated the arbitrary political use of permits. It was a casebook example of the difference between real and empty constitutional rights. City officials refused to engage in serious negotiations over permits until one week before the Convention, when we sued them in federal court. Until that time they pursued a stalling strategy, popular with city officials everywhere, designed to reduce numbers by shrouding the protest with uncertainty. This tactic is a direct attempt to emasculate substantive rights guaranteed by the First Amendment.

We proposed a series of demonstrations in Chicago that we felt would disrupt the ritual of a "Democratic Convention" and would show the reality behind it, but that would not physically interfere with the right of the Democrats to convene. In fact, the two major events we proposed were a free music Festival of Life as a human alternative to the inhuman political convention and a mass march to the Chicago Amphitheater on the night Humphrey was to be nominated. The city could easily have accommodated these events with little inconvenience and even less physical disruption. There was more than sufficient police capability to contain the large crowds that would gather alongside the Amphitheater, and while there would have been countless minor infractions of the law (littering, use of marijuana, and so forth) the scale would have been no greater than that of a large athletic event and far smaller than that which was tolerated in 1969 at Woodstock. There were, in fact, no serious constitutional "rights in conflict," as the title of the Walker Report later implied.

The city of Chicago's view of the First Amendment, on the other hand, implied that protest should reinforce the sense of weakness and prostration before authority implicit in the word "petition." So officials proposed meaningless rights of assembly. They rejected the proposed assembly at the Amphitheater on the grounds of "security" and "traffic congestion." They rejected the Festival of Life by declaring that during the week of the Convention they would enforce an 11 P.M. curfew as well as all local ordinances. In return, they offered a march through the Loop and a bandshell rally during the daylight hours of nomination day. Rennie's reply was that such a rally, instead of promoting protest, would have underscored people's helplessness in the face of a great national emergency. The negotiations over the meaning of the First Amendment then broke down.

The government made the familiar argument that we had framed our demands in such a way that they were "nonnegotiable," that we were not willing to compromise. We replied, in Rennie's words, that "we would negotiate anything but the Constitution," and, if that document was suspended in our case, we had what the Reverend Jesse Jackson testified was a "moral permit" to march anyway. We did not want or need a permit to be surrounded helplessly in a bandshell by troops. Instead, we would issue ourselves a permit based on rights that the government could not legitimately suspend under any circumstances.

(Even this step was not going "outside the law" but was going outside the arena of respectful protest. When the U.S. Supreme Court wanted to manipulate protest in the South, for instance, it justified exactly what we did in Chicago. It ruled that the Reverend Fred Shuttlesworth was justified in marching against an injunction in Birmingham, Alabama, because a permit was unlawfully denied his organization.)

Our speeches were not mere abstract "advocacy." Foran carefully stressed that we could have advocated anything. But neither were the speeches, in the language of the anti-riot law, illegal "incitement." For incitement to be illegal, there must be an existing prior peaceful and legal situation, in which First Amendment remedies are available for redress of grievances, that is deliberately shattered by speech and action. Obviously when speeches are given in the face of military occupation, they are inherently disruptive. They are not incitement to violence because violence has already been introduced into the situation. They are words of resistance, self-defense, and survival. Nor can "assemblies" be orderly or peaceful in an occupied city. Assemblies become inherently mobile and urgent if only to prevent encirclement by troops and mass arrest. The police clearing of Lincoln Park created our street tactics in Chicago. To avoid mass arrest, we called for people to move in "small groups," which police called "guerrilla war." To avoid a losing confrontation, which the media would ignore and the average citizen comfortably dismiss, we called for people to confront the police in front of the Hilton and in front of cameras, so that the gas and blood would be experienced by the entire Convention and the entire country. The police called this a "riot."

The main point is that the Chicago conflict could not be simplified, as it was in the press, to one of free speech versus respect for the law. By defining the question as one of free speech, many of our supporters were making a major liberal mistake. They opened themselves up to a common-sense conservative criticism: free speech is all right, but not obscene epithets shouted at police. Liberal sympathizers were being forced, in effect, to defend our right to shout "Fire!" in a crowded theater. In reality, the government, not the radical left, has become a "clear and present danger" to our common security. In this situation radical action has to be defended, not on the basis of civil liberties, but on the basis of the principles embodied in the Declaration of Independence.

VI

Their Identity on Trial

Putting our identity on trial caused our prosecutors to expose their own.

Normally in America oppressors appear to be flexible, even friendly persons. Only when their power is threatened are we given a glimpse of the paranoia, the rigidity, the violence at their core. This threat to power can occur with little or no provocation from those whom they oppress. The mere fact that the oppressed are becoming conscious of their own needs is enough to shake any system that for its maintenance depends primarily on attitudes of conformity and submission.

The American system, perhaps more than any other, controls people through manipulation rather than force. Advertising, the mass media, schools, electoral politics, the church, all serve to create a belief that this is the best of all possible societies, that no alternative ways of life are really achievable. Blacks, the Cubans, the Vietnamese, all are shattering the image that the world is one-dimensional, and now even white youth is creating a dimension of its own. In this conflict, our identity itself is the alternative, reaching people on a deeper level than rhetoric or blueprints ever could. We are living proof that life can be different. Our very existence, therefore, is a threat to the social order. *Our appearance, because we strip away all illusion, produces the total revelation of our oppressors as well.*

According to the testimony of Norman Mailer:

. . . It was Rubin's view that the military-industrial Establishment was so full of secret horror and guilt that they would crack at the slightest provocation. . . . The presence of 100,000 young people in Chicago at a festival with rock bands would thoroughly intimidate and terrify the Establishment, particularly the Johnson-Vietnam war establishment, that Lyndon Johnson would have to be nominated under armed guard . . . and Rubin said: *I think the beauty of it is that the Establishment is going to do it all themselves, we won't do a thing. We are just going to be there and they won't be able to take it. They will smash the city themselves, they will provoke all the violence. . . .*

This may be why we have been confronted through the years with a system that seemed sophisticated until the very moment when sophistication was needed most: the moment of showdown. Then it produced true-to-form villains: Bull Connor as the Southern cop, Clark Kerr as the bureaucratic administrator, Robert McNamara as the military computer, Lewis Hershey as the draft man, Lyndon Johnson and Richard Nixon as the politicians. The system is flexible, even benign, when it can afford to be, but its real protectors seem to step forward at every moment of serious crisis. These villains, then, are not isolated and unique persons but necessary guardians of the Establishment.

From the very first moment of our arraignment we realized that our fates were to be decided by a madman, Judge Julius J. Hoffman. Some say that if Julius Hoffman did not exist, we would have had to invent him. This assumes wrongly that we enjoy being held under irrational domination. More accurately, we could say that a country invents the authorities it deserves. Of course, not everyone in America deserves Julius J. Hoffman, but he does represent perfectly the decaying aristocracy of dinosaurs we see everywhere, directing universities, corporations, and draft boards. Though he is slightly older, he is only a senior member of the same imperial generation. He is a younger man, for example, than the Speaker of the House of Representatives and about the same age as ten of their twenty-one committee chairmen. He is younger by ten years than the judge who presided at the trial of Dr. Spock. He is an over-assimilated Midwestern Jew, a man who married into wealth, a director of the Brunswick Corporation, which manufactures materiel for Vietnam, a resident of Chicago's exclusive Gold Coast.

Perhaps the most striking fact about Julius Hoffman is that he has carried on arrogantly for fifteen years without censure from the government or the legal profession. Virtually every member of the Illinois bar with whom we spoke called Judge Hoffman a "hanging judge." Yet they accepted him without protest. A University of Chicago law professor, writing after the trial, said it was "common knowledge that this judge callously and insistently degrades and provokes the lawyers who happen to appear before him unless they come from the office of the United States Attorney. . . ."

During the trial, we had occasion to see firsthand the groveling of attorneys who appeared for matters as simple as a postponement. Literally bowing before Judge Hoffman, smiling humbly, and begging mercy for their clients, these attorneys were without self-respect; looking back, their timidity made Bill Kunstler and Len Weinglass appear in contrast to be totally disrespectful and defiant.

The entire Chicago bar apparently permitted Judge Hoffman to become the monster that he is. To practice successfully in Chicago, goes the conventional wisdom, a lawyer needs a good reputation among the judges before whom he appears. Otherwise, both practice and clients suffer. Any disrespect displayed before Judge Hoffman would be a mark on one's reputation and would be taken as an attack on the whole judiciary. Therefore, play along with the old bastard, say the lawyers in their offices, and build up the firm. This prevailing acceptance of Judge Hoffman makes nearly every member of the profession in Chicago a silent accomplice in the growth of that judge's abusive power.

More important is the fact that the U.S. government would rely on Judge Hoffman to try this case. Had the government any desire to produce even the semblance of a fair trial, it could have sought to bring the case before almost anyone else. But not only did the government proceed with Julius Hoffman; it never even objected to the severity or the irrationality of his rulings. In fact, it toadied to him. Schultz congratulated him for withstanding several months of harassment, and Foran remarked at the trial's end: "Judge Hoffman is a strict judge. I like strict judges myself."

(Confirmation of this came from Roger Wilkins, one of our witnesses, who was at the Gridiron Club festivities a few weeks after the trial. Wilkins found himself the only black person [besides the "Mayor" of Washington] at an event at which Nixon and Agnew played "Dixie" and the largest standing ovations went to Clement Haynsworth—and Julius J. Hoffman. At about the same time, the judge was welcomed at a White House reception.)

Julius Hoffman is symbolic, then, of an entire class. He is not an accident, not a vestige of the past, but a perfect representative of a class of dinosaurs that is vengefully striking out against the future. Hoffman's vanity, arrogance, racism, paternalism, indifference to official violence, and blindness are the primary features of that class.

Although the government's representatives were overshadowed in the trial by the judge, they nevertheless played their own roles to perfection.

Tom Foran represented the U.S. government for the northern district of Illinois. A short, squat man in a tight-fitting gabardine suit, he was struggling to retain his 1940s Golden Gloves fighting form. Someone said Foran was Jack Armstrong. Stew Albert, an underground writer, decided he was a repressed and frightened homosexual. The point is the same: Foran represented the conventional image of manhood to the jury—a fighter, a father of six, earthly but intelligent, still vaguely handsome, knowledgeable in the ways of the world, but struggling as a Catholic to retain purity. He was the sort of man whose apparent politeness conceals a vulgar rage, as we learned from his speech to an athletic booster meeting after the trial. There Foran said he had kept his sanity during the trial by attending wrestling matches on Sundays. He called Abbie "scummy but clever," Dave Dellinger a "sneak," Jerry Rubin a "punk."

Foran was a Democratic appointee of Mayor Daley's who had previously made his money in urban-renewal dealings. When we first met him during our arraignment, Foran had a few liberal markings compared to his colleagues. For instance, he argued—against the judge's will—that we be permitted to travel and speak in the months between the arraignment and the trial. At the judge's request we negotiated an agreement in Foran's office, and he gave in quickly on the issue rather than provoke a fight over free speech and travel that would be sure to damage him politically.

But Foran was otherwise locked into a dogmatic position, not only because of his role as prosecutor but because he was central to the very events of Chicago's Convention Week that the trial was about. During the summer of 1968, he had generally refused to help in permit negotiations and, as we would discover after the trial a year later, had been present at Michigan and Balbo on the night of the great police attack on the demonstrators. Although he termed that attack an "anarchist riot" during the trial, he spoke approvingly of it in his first post-trial speech.

So Foran embodied a fact we could never get into evidence: that we could not have a fair trial when the prosecutor himself was the real perpetrator of the violence. Foran, perhaps more than anyone else in the courtroom, had a precise knowledge of the city's attitude toward protest; of the police instructions at the time of the Convention; and of the methods by which our indictments were arrived at. Yet he could sit in court extolling the "adversary system" as the best means of getting at the truth.

Foran was skilled at committing outrageous legal offenses in a cool and subtle way, similar in craft to a crooked card dealer. He would manage to scorn our lawyers by laughing under his breath each time he objected. He glared, muttered, and shook his head at our witnesses as they testified. He gave slight affirmative or negative nods to signal his witnesses about their answers. In this way too he was a perfect symbol of the fact that law masks repression.

Richard Schultz was the ideal apprentice prosecutor. Young, bespectacled, and physically awkward, he is a perfectionist with an uncontrollable personal ambition. If Foran was the body of the prosecution, Schultz was the brain. Schultz was an overcharged computer, a structure freak who knew the exact details of "criminal" meetings we had long since forgotten. He seemed to live inside the world of facts that he had constructed from his interviews with agents. The geometric rationality of this world was paranoid. Everything necessarily had to have a deliberate cause and, where we were involved, a disruptive one. "Nothing Mr. Kunstler does is involuntary," he declared one day. At another point he charged that we were "coaching" our witnesses, most of whom had never testified in a court before, to deliberately act confused on the stand. And during a conflict over where we should go to the toilet, he confessed to losing his temper and "succumbing" to our tactic of harassment, "the same tactic they've been using on police and authorities *all their lives.*" Bobby Seale's demand to represent himself was for Schultz "nothing but a ploy" to "create error on the record," and the bringing of Ramsey Clark to testify was only a "gimmick" to use the former Attorney General's prestige on our behalf.

Schultz actually was the immediate provocateur of the sharpest disruptions of the trial. The first was the gagging of Bobby Seale. Before court on the day of the gagging, Bobby entered and addressed some Panthers in the presence of Schultz. He told them, "You know I have a constitutional right to defend myself; you know I'm standing on this right. Now you know the party has a policy of defending ourselves when and if we're attacked, but today, if anything happens, you be cool, hear, you be cool." Then when Judge Hoffman arrived a few moments later, Schultz found it necessary to tell him: "If the Court please, before you came into this courtroom, if the Court please, Bobby Seale stood up and addressed this group, and Bobby Seale said that if he were attacked, they knew what to do. . . . He was talking to those people about an attack by them." The result was the pandemonium that ended in Bobby's being taken away and gagged and all the defendants being charged with contempt.

A second major incident provoked by Schultz was his move to prevent Ramsey Clark from testifying. The potential appearance of the former Attorney General obviously upset the new Justice Department, but we were not prepared for the extent of its rage. What mattered evidently was not the conflict between the new and old Justice Departments, but the fact that Ramsey Clark's appearance would be so damaging to the government's case. If the Attorney General in office at the time of the Convention did not seem to consider us criminals, then the whole prosecution would be exposed as a purely political affair and might cause "reasonable doubt" of our guilt in the minds of the jury.

When we interviewed Clark at his Falls Church, Virginia, home two days before his appearance, there were two representatives of the new Justice Department present. One described himself as the "eyes and ears" and said rather ominously that he'd seen me before. Later Bill Kunstler recalled having tried a civil-rights case against him in Mississippi four years ago. As the agent took notes, Clark related the substance of his possible testimony. It was more or less favorable to us:

1. Clark was publicly critical of Mayor Daley's shoot-to-kill order.

2. Daley's office opposed permits. The Justice Department officials were impressed by Rennie Davis' cooperation but could find no constructive elements in Chicago to pressure the city to negotiate.

3. When Chicago requested 5000 pre-positioned troops one week before the Convention, Clark opposed the move.

4. Clark turned down FBI requests for authorization to wiretap our communications.

5. During Convention Week, Wesley Pomeroy told Clark by phone that he was ashamed to be a policeman after witnessing the Chicago police in action.

6. Clark called Foran after the Convention and suggested an investigation of police brutality but no grand-jury investigation of the demonstrators.

After our interview, and while Bill Kunstler was momentarily out of the room, the Justice Department agents attempted to persuade Clark not to testify on the grounds that he would be "used." He told them it was his duty to testify to whatever was relevant, but when he came to Chicago two days later the same agents were present and had reported to Schultz and Foran about the interview. Before Clark was called to testify, Schultz rose to warn Judge Hoffman of what was about to happen. Schultz read a twisted version of the interview, then suggested that Clark not be allowed to testify. Schultz's reasoning was adopted from *1984*: according to Schultz, the Attorney General could not testify to certain confidential matters, especially those having to do with "national security." The government could wiretap and infiltrate our meetings, he was saying, but we could not hear evidence from a top participant in theirs. Furthermore, the rest of Clark's testimony, said Schultz, would be "cumulative" because Clark's assistants, Roger Wilkins and Wesley Pomeroy, had already testified to meetings with Rennie Davis. (When Wilkins and Pomeroy were on the stand, however, Schultz had objected to placing in evidence a memo about Wilkins' positive evaluation of Davis and negative evaluations of the city. All we were allowed to state then was that the meeting between Wilkins, Pomeroy, and Davis had occurred. The evaluations by the Justice Department were dismissed as "hearsay opinion" not subject to cross-examination.)

So Schultz concluded that the only reason Clark was being called was as a "prestige witness" and that the government would be made to "look bad" by objecting to his testimony in front of the jury. Letting Clark testify would contribute to the "mockery" we were trying to create. The judge agreed. And then a final nail was driven in: the lawyers and defendants were ordered not to say anything about this suppression to the jury.

The New York Times saw this as "the ultimate outrage" of the trial. Our feelings were even stronger. A day later, after Foran made a pious statement about the government's "fairness." I exploded to Foran (while the jury was going out of the room): "Fantastic. You wouldn't even let the former Attorney General testify." The judge did not hear the exchange, or at least did not react until Schultz and Foran came to the lectern to put the "outburst" on the record. For good measure, they claimed I had jumped up and had screamed the words.

The *Times* said the Clark incident proved the determination of the Justice Department to win a conspiracy conviction at any cost. For us, it was only part of a pattern of hysterical repressiveness that began with the arraignment.

VII

The Rigging of Justice

Our twenty-four pre-trial motions were designed to challenge the fairness of the law and the trial procedures. We asked to inspect the grand-jury minutes on the transcript and to disqualify Judge Hoffman. We asked that the indictment be dismissed because of the unconstitutionality of the law; because of its generality; because of bias in the grand jury; because of irregularities in the selection of the grand jury; and on the grounds of double jeopardy. We asked that our attorneys be allowed to conduct a *voir dire* of the jury—a direct inquiry into their social attitudes. All the motions were denied.

In the light of later events, the most significant motion was a request to postpone the trial for six weeks so that Charles Garry could recover from an operation and become chief trial counsel, and counsel for Bobby Seale in particular. The government argued that the trial should go ahead without Garry, that the motion was simply a ploy to gain a delay. The motion was denied.

The first several days of the trial served as an introduction to the unbelievable treatment to which we would be subjected in the months that followed. Despite the absence of his lawyer, Bobby was told that he could not represent himself. On a technicality—because he had signed papers to see Bobby—Bill Kunstler was told that he would therefore be Bobby's attorney. On a further technicality—because they sent telegrams of withdrawal instead of making personal appearances—four of our pre-trial lawyers were arrested, brought in handcuffs to Chicago, and jailed. Len Weinglass was held in contempt of court for persisting in making opening remarks that were far less "opinionated" than those offered by Schultz. That plus the evident insanity of the judge made it clear to us that this trial was more of a railroading than we had believed possible. From then on we knew that our activity would have to be designed not to show the truth but to show how truth was prohibited from entering the courtroom.

The rigging was always done in the name of the law. "The adversary system has been developed for 500 years," Foran said (later modifying the figure to 200). "It's the best way of determining the truth and we're not going to change it for these defendants." Everything was done also to "protect our rights," like refusing Bobby Seale's request to defend himself, eventually refusing permission for us to leave the room, and so on. Listening to this day after day enabled us to understand the process of brainwashing. The repetition had an effect. For instance, Len began to believe that the form of his questions *might* be objectionable, and he had to return to the law library to reassure himself that it wasn't. The rest of us finally began to accept the rigging as normal and lost our sense of outrage. The fact that the judge sustained almost all the government's hundreds of objections finally no longer disturbed us. We shrugged at visitors to the courtroom, who invariably left with the same reaction of wondering how we could "take it." These famous "rules of evidence," we discovered, might be valuable for judging the cause of an automobile accident, but they were a total obstruction to sifting the political evidence at the heart of our case.

Even though our states of mind were being prosecuted, we could not offer any evidence as to our true intent, opinions, or feelings as they had been in 1968. Our feelings about the war, racism, and cultural decadence, so necessary to an ex-

planation of our intent in coming to Chicago, were never allowed. Simply to demonstrate what was blocked from testimony, at the end of our defense we presented several expert
witnesses to explore the question of our intent in coming to
Chicago. Congressman John Conyers testified, without the
jury present, to the racist character of the Democratic Party;
Frank Bardacke discussed the repression of the emerging
youth culture; Peter Martinson discussed his own role in torturing Vietnamese (to which he had testified at the International War Crimes Tribunal); and Staughton Lynd testified
about parallels between the American resistance against the
British Empire in the eighteenth century and our resistance
against the American government in the late 1960s. Their
collective testimony was considered "irrelevant" despite the
fact that each of them had associations with the defendants
and could testify about the effect of the war, racism, and
other issues on our consciousness.

Nor was it possible to produce the public documents, written and circulated in 1968, that dealt with our intentions in
coming to Chicago. Two documents excluded, for instance,
were the Justice Department memorandum containing a positive evaluation of the Mobilization's plans, and an article
written by Abbie in *The Realist* calling people to Chicago
and explaining his own perspective. The government could
cross-examine on excerpts from the article ("Didn't you plan
public fornication?"), but we could not place the whole article before the jury. Nor could we introduce Abbie's books
Revolution for the Hell of It and *Woodstock Nation.* Also
blocked were a twenty-five page position paper written by
Rennie and myself covering every aspect of our own Chicago
plans, and a long memo detailing our intentions that was
submitted to city officials as part of our permit application.
The basis of the government's objection was that the documents were all "self-serving." (The usual situation in which
this rule is applied is when a bank robber leaves notes proclaiming his innocence with a few friends before he pulls the

job, not when organizational documents are circulated in public.) If Chicago officials really believed we had secret plans for which our publicly circulated documents were merely "window-dressing," why didn't they undermine us by granting permits?

The totality of the repression during Convention Week—for example, against newsmen and McCarthy-Kennedy workers—was also "immaterial to the charges in the indictment." We attempted to introduce evidence depicting the frustrations of permit negotiations conducted by the McCarthy movement; motions made on the floor of the Convention to recess and move to another city; marches made by delegates in which arrests and civil disobedience took place; beatings and detention of delegates on the Convention floor; the wholesale attack on cameramen in Lincoln Park. All of this was rejected. "The McCarthy people are not on trial here, Your Honor," was the response.

Finally, we were never allowed to explore the intentions and pre-Convention planning of the other party to the case, the government of the United States of America. We were permitted to deny the charges against ourselves but not to put our defense in the context of the Chicago police state and the Democratic Party's electoral planning. An exploration of the intent of the other side was again held to be either "immaterial" or "hearsay" or a violation of "national security." Some examples of the evidence the jury was thus prevented from hearing are as follows.

Our first witness, Dr. Edward J. Sparling, president emeritus of Roosevelt University, could have testified to the report of a commission he chaired that criticized city permit negotiations and police brutality during the April 1968 peace march that foreshadowed the Convention. The report warned that a different approach should be taken toward the Convention protests coming up in August of that year. Our intent in coming to Chicago was influenced to a large degree by what had occurred that April.

• Justice Department officials could have testified much more extensively about the nature and content of their meetings with Rennie Davis, Mayor Daley, and national officials.

• Because Judge Hoffman would not rule him a "hostile witness," Mayor Daley did not have to answer any questions at all about his pre-Convention decisions.

• Richard Goodwin could have told how he tried, and failed, to persuade Daley and Humphrey to take a constructive attitude toward demonstrations in the city.

• The testimony of Chicago attorney Robert Downs and author John Sack, who were among police during the Convention battles, was not admitted. Downs heard police slapping their weapons and eagerly discussing the clubbing of hippies when they were about to clear the park. Sack saw police unaffected, even laughing, about the term "pigs," and about the pitiful objects, like shoes, that were thrown at them.

• National Guardsman Richard Gillette was with soldiers who brought their private loaded weapons to Chicago riot duty to "kill the hippies," but he was not allowed to report this to the jury.

• Renault ("Reggie") Robinson, a Chicago police officer who was the chairman of the Afro-American Patrolmen's League, had some of the most explosive testimony that was suppressed. He listened to police chanting "Kill, kill, kill" in pre-Convention drills, and knew of cases in which black patrolmen had refused to participate in the bloodletting. After the Convention he was present at a police "victory party" at which a captain stood at attention while his men shouted "Sieg heil."

VIII

On Contempt of Court

No issue in the Conspiracy trial has been more misunderstood than that of our being held in contempt. Politicians, judges, and lawyers—and above all, the mass media—have outrageously exaggerated the courtroom confrontations. Our behavior has been described as violent and anarchic, part of a new conspiracy to stop the courts from functioning. The Yippies have enjoyed and fed this overreaction because they like to provoke apoplexy in their elders.

But the facts regarding our contempt of court are quite different from the myths. Time and again we were provoked into choosing between speaking out or becoming meek, silent accomplices to our own prosecution. Dave Dellinger set forth our common feelings at the end of the trial when he was sentenced for contempt:

DELLINGER: The first two contempts concerned the Moratorium and Bobby Seale, the two issues that the country refuses to solve, refuses to take seriously.
THE COURT: Get to the subject of punishment and I will be glad to hear you. I don't want you to talk politics.
DELLINGER: You see, that's one of the reasons I have needed to stand up and speak anyway, because you have tried to keep what you call politics, which means the truth, out of this courtroom, just as the prosecution has . . .
THE COURT: I will ask you to sit down . . .
DELLINGER: Therefore it is necessary . . .

THE COURT: I won't let you go any further . . .

DELLINGER: You wanted us to be like good Germans, supporting the evils of our decade, and when we refused to be good Germans, and came to Chicago and demonstrated, despite the threats and intimidation of the Establishment, now you want us to be like good Jews going quietly and politely to the concentration camps while you and this court suppress freedom and the truth. People will no longer be quiet, people are going to speak up. I am an old man, and I am just speaking feebly and not too well, but I reflect the spirit that will echo . . .

THE COURT: Take him out.

DELLINGER: . . . throughout the world.

[*Disorder*]

Contempt of court ordinarily refers to physical attempts to disrupt or delay the "administration of justice," such as when a defendant throws a chair at a witness or acts in some way to prevent a trial from occurring. Myth has it that we regularly tore apart the courtroom, that our slogan "Stop the Trial" meant stop it by forcible means. But a look at the record of 175 contempt citations shows that nearly all of them were for words rather than deeds.

There were a small number of theatrical events that neither delayed nor disrupted the trial: bringing a birthday cake to Bobby Seale (which was stopped in the hallway); bringing U.S. and Vietnamese flags into the courtroom before the session began; and wearing judicial robes at the end of the trial. But the only physical violence that involved defendants during the five months occurred in conjunction with the chaining of Bobby Seale and the revocation of Dave Dellinger's bail. On these two occasions it was the arbitrary rulings of the judge and the physical attacks of the U.S. marshals that caused our "contempt," our resistance. The other moments of violence—perhaps five in all—took place between marshals and those spectators who could not adjust quickly enough to the totalitarian decorum of Judge Hoffman's courtroom.

Our "contempt," then, was present more in our attitudes than in our actions. We never respected the court. We mocked it in press conferences, demonstrations, and speeches from the beginning of the trial. Both judge and prosecutor saw this mockery in the papers and on television. Since they could not punish us for exercising freedom of speech outside the courtroom, they chose to punish us for any evidence of disrespect we let slip inside the court. Nearly all these occasions of disrespect were *spontaneous* reactions against government lies or violations of our rights. Few of them disrupted the proceedings, and in fact, what seemed to concern the government more was the disruption we were causing to the *image* of American justice. Most of all, the record of our contempt can be read as a record of assaults on the vanity and authority of Judge Julius J. Hoffman.

Even one of our critics accepted much of this view after reading the transcript of the contempt sentencing. Harry Kalven, a Chicago law professor who debated with Bill Kunstler during the trial, later discovered that there were "stretches of the trial during which few, if any, contempts arose" and that "over one hundred of the contempts have occurred within sixteen trial days of the five-month trial." And he concluded:

I am impressed, contrary to the impressions I had gotten from the press coverage, by the sense that the interruptions were in no sense random events and that two or three triggering events, such as the handling of Seale and the revocation of Dellinger's bond, account for the major part of the troubles. . . . The incidence of unrest seems not easily compatible with the notion that the defendants and counsel relentlessly and steadily pursued a single-minded strategy of disturbing the trial process.

Kalven's judgment that there was no unified conspiracy in our contempt cannot be stressed too strongly.

Each defendant reacted in a different way.

Bobby Seale's "contempt" arose because of the judge's arbitrary refusal to delay the trial until Charles Garry was well, and his further refusal to let Bobby defend himself. This left

Bobby with little choice. Seized in the night and moved to Chicago, facing a possible death sentence in Connecticut, what was he to do? Accept the legal counsel of two attorneys, Bill Kunstler and Len Weinglass, whom he had never seen before? Accept his enslaved status during the Chicago trial while an appeal was being heard in higher courts?

He believed this would mean abandoning his right to a fair trial altogether. Instead his response was to stand in a disciplined way on rights that he correctly believed could not be legally suspended, constitutional rights that were supposedly guaranteed to black people during Reconstruction. Those laws, established through civil war, ensured the right of black people to equal protection under the law in white society. All of Bobby's "disruption" revolved around these contested rights. He stood or spoke only when his name arose in testimony or when evidence was introduced against him.

Unlike the other defendants, Bobby did not have the alternative of expressing his views in press conferences or speeches. He came to Chicago in chains, bound for Connecticut. The courtroom was his only forum, speaking there his only opportunity to break through the tissue of lies and stereotypes about the Black Panthers. The threat of severance from the trial or a contempt sentence was small, since Bobby was already expecting a long jail term. So his "contempt" was necessary to his legal defense and freedom of speech.

The goal was to create a trial within a trial to bring particular attention to the frame-up of Bobby and to build national support for the Panthers before his upcoming trial in Connecticut. Bobby wanted both ourselves and Panthers in the courtroom to keep the focus on himself, remaining cool under provocation. We were to avoid having our bail revoked, if possible, using our limited freedom to educate and organize people around the issues he was raising.

This decision was to cause controversy later because many people felt we should not have gone ahead with the trial after the gagging and severance of Bobby. What actually happened was that we accumulated a full *one-third* of our total contempt citations during the three days Bobby was gagged, but we were physically and politically unable to stop the gagging. Even refusing to go on with the trial would have been symbolic because the trial would have continued anyway. Inside the courtroom we were powerless against that armed and ruthless machine. Only a massive political movement, which we have yet to build, could strike down Bobby's contempt sentence and liberate him from prison.

In the meantime, Bobby's act of courage has exposed and threatened the courts perhaps more than any single act in American judicial history. Bobby was following the Panthers' political tradition of expressing the right of black people to self-determination. Huey P. Newton had tested whether self-defense in the streets was constitutionally guaranteed to blacks, and Bobby was testing the same issue in the courtroom.

Dave Dellinger's "contempt" was the result of his militant nonviolent temperament. After thirty years of struggle, the radical pacifist philosophy of "speaking truth to power" and the strategy of awakening the social conscience through civil disobedience have become completely natural to Dave's personality. As long ago as World War II, for instance, he refused to register as a conscientious objector (even though a divinity-school deferment was possible); when he was released after a year in jail, he again refused to register for CO status and was penalized with another one-year term.

An analysis of his contempt citations in our trial reveals a spontaneous refusal to countenance even the smallest hypocrisy. When Foran claimed that Dave had planned the Moratorium "disruption" on the elevator in the Federal Building in Chicago, Dave's reply was typical: "I don't mind your making all of those objections. When you start lying about me, though, I think that is disgusting." At another point, Dave found it necessary to say: "I beg your pardon—I did not utter a single noise; when I have noises I stand up and say so."

Dave's spontaneous utterances ("Oh, Jesus"; "Ridiculous") finally led to his loss of bail when he reacted to a police witness' accusation of violence on his part with: "Oh, bullshit, that is an absolute lie. Let's argue about what I stand for and what you stand for but let's not make up things like that."

Dave's more eloquent responses followed the theme of refusing to be a good German: "Decorum is more important than justice, I suppose," he said. "Just walk politely into jail." Dave's personal experience in prison during World War II also affected his attitude. At that time the judge and the prosecutor had termed him a sincere, dedicated young man, ahead of his times, but as soon as the jail doors closed on him he was thrown up against the wall. He was never again going to be polite for the sake of an illusory effectiveness.

THE COURT: I have never sat in fifty years through a trial where a party to a lawsuit called the judge a liar.
DELLINGER: Maybe they were afraid to go to jail rather than tell the truth, but I would rather go to jail for however long you send me than to let you get away with that kind of thing, and people not realize what you are doing.

We were all shocked when *Rennie* got two-and-a-half years. During most of the trial he was a relatively mild-mannered defendant and was especially soft-spoken on the witness stand. But Rennie was sentenced to ten months on contempt charges for his performance *as a witness.* (Abbie, by contrast, violated every conceivable custom on the stand but received few contempt citations for his performance.) Rennie's contempt on the stand involved, first, remarking that the judge was asleep; second, stating that the judge had not read a document that was handed up in evidence; and third, trying to put his answers into context, instead of giving a simple yes or no answer. The rest of Rennie's "contempts" came at a few spontaneous moments, such as when he told

Bobby that the marshals had taken his birthday cake, or when he felt a moral obligation. ("Ladies and gentlemen of the jury, it's terrible, they're torturing Bobby Seale when you're out of the room.") Rennie seems to have been penalized for being so good. He was always the most clean-cut and responsible of the eight, whether in the Mobe or the Conspiracy office, and was constantly referred to in the press as a "4-H type" and "the boy next door." He came across that way to the Justice Department investigators in 1968 and on the witness stand in 1969. The cross-examination of Rennie, Foran said, was the hardest of his life. The government was frustrated: Rennie did not fit its image of a violent, pro-Vietcong revolutionary. Schultz acknowledged it all one day when he lost his temper and accused Rennie of having a "split personality."

Maybe Abbie understood it best when he said that the Mobe—with its structure, its staff, its marshals, its office, its program, and with Rennie as a "face man"—must have seemed serious and probably guilty compared to the Yippies. Rennie paid for being the organization man of the Conspiracy.

For *Abbie* and *Jerry,* on the other hand, the courtroom was a new theater, perhaps a purer kind of theater than anything in previous Yippie history. More than any of the other defendants, they wanted to create the *image* of a courtroom shambles. The setting could not have been more perfect: daily performances before a press gallery hungry for sensational news. Part of the Yippie genius is to manipulate the fact that the media will always emphasize the bizarre. Even the straightest reporter will communicate chaos because it sells. The Yippies know this because their politics involve consciously marketing themselves as mythic personality models for young kids. Now almost entirely media personalities, Abbie and Jerry would spend much of their courtroom time analyzing trial coverage in the papers, plotting press conferences, arranging for "Yippie witnesses" to get on the stand in time for the deadlines, and even calculating which of the defendants was getting most of the media attention. They knew that the smallest unconventional act would goad the court into overreaction, would be fixed upon by the press, and would spread an image of defiance and disorder to the country. The defiance would enthuse young people, the "disorder" would panic parents into greater paranoia, and the repression-rebellion cycle would increase in every home and school.

The Yippies believed in confrontations in which they would risk jail attempting to make the government back down. When Dave's bail was revoked near the end of the trial, for instance, it was the Yippies who pushed hardest for a deliberate disruption that would land all the defendants in jail. It was their feeling that our being jailed together would help Dave get out and would create the right image to mobilize people for action at the trial's end. The next day they tried to implement this strategy, screaming a stream of epithets at the judge, the likes of which he had not heard for the full four months of the trial. Instead of rising to the provocation, however, as he had done on many minor occasions before, the judge would not play along; he was satisfied merely to record the contempts in his doomsday book.

In the end, the two were treated as distinctly different individuals: Jerry got two-and-a-half years for contempt, Abbie only eight months. Perhaps it was the judge's error in counting; nevertheless, it recalled the old gap between them— Jerry had been characterized as the "militant," Abbie as the "flower child." Compared to Abbie, Jerry's image as a Yippie was neither funny nor delightful. It was that of a hostile revolutionary, a more serious, nervous, even guilty person in the courtroom. Jerry's endless needling of the prosecution seemed designed to hurt their feelings, while Abbie was never dislikable. His mockery usually left the government not simply upset but laughing at itself and wondering if he was serious. Abbie is a kind of contemporary Voltaire who charms the very ruling class he threatens. He will be murdered by a right-wing lunatic, not by the "liberal" CIA.

John and *Lee* stayed out of direct contempt situations for the most part, perhaps because they were framed in the first place and saw little percentage in being punished further when they might be found innocent on the main charges. Though he occasionally lost his temper, John was respectful all the time. Even in his moments of contempt, he made his statements politely. Yet in the end he received a seven-month sentence. Lee hardly spoke in the courtroom. Instead, he exercised a unique form of contempt, a withdrawal into the *I Ching* and assorted sociology and science-fiction texts. Lee was ahead in two ways: he lived there while in court, and he shared the American underground's fear of never getting out of jail once behind bars. The wonder is that he almost never lost control of what he told the judge was a "quiet rage."

Of all the defendants, I probably advocated the most careful line of behavior in the courtroom. One reason was to cultivate support within our jury of middle-aged Americans. My own hopes for the jury were perhaps higher than those of any other defendant (I once believed we had a potential base of eight among the twelve!). And I believed that a verdict of acquittal for some and a hung jury for others would do more to disrupt the legal machinery of repression than any spontaneous act in court. It seemed possible to bring our life style and politics into the courtroom in ways calculated to educate the sympathetic jurors, without casting ourselves as the provocateurs of Judge Hoffman.

My more basic difference was with the ideas of "moral witness" and "theater" at the root of both the pacifist and Yippie politics. These principles can effectively expose institutions but can never prevent repression and punishment; as Abbie said, the trial would be "a victory every day until the last." Then we would be sentenced for contempt. We could strip away the authority of the judge and prosecution but not their power. So it seemed a senseless sacrifice to accumulate prison time for spontaneous outbursts. But the graver danger was that we would be denied bail and held in prison during the time of appeals, thus cutting off our right to speak and organize. Since we were entering a period of repression in which the higher courts were unreliable, it seemed best to keep our distance from the closing jaws of the state. With the state becoming totalitarian, moral witness was masochistic, and theater a bad joke. A disciplined strategy seemed necessary: a minimum of legitimate resistance in the courtroom, a spectacular political defense, and massive speaking and organizing campaigns around the country. Exposure of the judiciary was possible, as in Huey's case, without volunteering for contempt citations.

There was no exit from confrontation, however. With a flexible and rational judge, it could have been avoided, but Julius Hoffman guaranteed it. He made it necessary for Bobby Seale, who was already in jail, to use the courtroom as his only forum. The absurdity of our cooperating with a madman like the judge forced everyone, including myself, to react to the situation in which we had been placed. Most of my contempt citations occurred with respect to the treatment of Bobby and the exclusion of the testimony of Ramsey Clark.

In the end, Dave and Abbie were right in their argument that a symbolic stand would move people. Our differences didn't matter, since the contempt sentences were to be served concurrently with the five-year sentences. My own contempt sentence, fifteen months, was the highest in relation to the number of citations (eleven).

The contempt sentences against *Bill* and *Lennie* had nothing whatever to do with disruption or obstruction. They were found in contempt because they tried to represent us

as we were instead of molding us into respectable defendants.

Before the trial neither had been a political radical. Bill
was so much the "liberal" that he voted for Humphrey in
1968. His legal practice for the Movement was primarily in
the South, where he relied on the liberalism of the higher
courts in battles with Southern judges. Len's political background involved some modest work for the Democratic Party
and a number of housing and welfare cases after we met in
Newark several years ago. A trip to Cuba was perhaps his
most unorthodox political act before the trial. He takes a
rather cynical view of "mass movements" and has defined his
work as a case-by-case effort to win individual justice.

The trial caused both to make choices. They found they
could not function within the protection of the higher courts,
nor could they behave in conventional ways in the courtroom.

The law, like politics, is organized around a principle of
"representation" rather than direct participation by the people most affected. The citizen is reduced to being a client. He
exercises choice only when he selects a lawyer. The lawyer
then takes over as the expert in how best to represent his
client's interests. The lawyer speaks for the client not in the
particular style of that individual but in a proper and formal-
ized way. Within this ritualized situation, the lawyer's highest
obligation is not to the client but to the legal system itself. As
a sworn "officer of the court," the lawyer is obliged to accept
the judge as the "governor of the trial."

Such a game might be effective in a criminal trial in which
the primary object is to win no matter what happens to the
truth. But when politics and identity are on trial and a
client's state of mind is the crime, a lawyer tends to become
part of the political confrontation. In our case, the lawyers
had an obligation to be officers in the court of a madman,
while making a vigorous defense of our revolutionary poli-

tics. For following their obligations to represent us Bill and
Len were held in contempt.

For adopting our spirit of equality in decision-making they
were called "mouthpieces" by Foran. The judge went even
further at the time of sentencing. Not once, he declared, did
either lawyer tell Bobby Seale to "cool it." This failure to act
as officers of the court, the judge felt, was part of a pattern of
conduct that is causing the national crime rate to rise. As he
put it: "Waiting in the wings are lawyers who are willing to
go beyond professional responsibility in their defense of a defendant." Nothing proves so well the fact that the lawyers'
contempt citations were for what they did *not* do. They did
not disrupt the court once. They refused to act as our custo-
dians or as disciplinarians for the judge.

Thus, as the legal nightmare unfolded, Bill and Len became themselves like defendants. Their hair grew longer
(though Len broke down and had a haircut at one crucial
moment). They became accustomed to sleeping in large communal apartments, and they gradually came to share our political conclusions about the law.

Bill especially went through a personal crisis whenever the
courtroom disintegrated into a raw human experience. His
years of politics have given him an accommodating surface
that not everyone likes, but he could not maintain this carefully polished exterior as the ordeal intensified. When his old
comrade, Ralph Abernathy, was prevented from testifying
because he arrived a few minutes late, Bill dropped his courtroom manner: "I have sat here for four-and-a-half months
and watched the objections sustained by Your Honor, and I
know this is not a fair trial. I know it in my heart. If I have to
lose my license to practice law, and if I have to go to jail, I
can't think of a better cause than to tell Your Honor that you
are doing a disservice to the law in saying we can't have
Ralph Abernathy on the stand. . . . Everything I've learned
in my life has come to naught. There is no law in the
court. . . ."

When the marshals dragged Dave's daughter and other spectators away during the sentencing, Bill dissolved into his human essence. He broke down and begged to be jailed: "Mine now, Judge, please. Please, I beg you. Come to mine. Do me too. I don't want to be out."

Len's courtroom behavior was far more restrained and correct than Bill's, yet he was called "wild man Weinglass" by the threatened judge. His acting in the way a model lawyer is expected to act was "disruptive" because it exposed the unfairness of the whole procedure and the impossibility of soothing the judge. Unlike Foran and Schultz, who relied on the judge's rulings rather than on prepared legal arguments, Len always worked to prepare case law for arguments that were always dismissed. Len's repeated questions about the different kinds of treatment accorded to government and defense drew no legal replies but only stern warnings from the judge. At the end of the trial, the judge still mispronounced Len's name, even as he was sentencing him:

THE COURT: Since you tell me this is your first case in a federal court . . . you will get along better by being respectful.
WEINGLASS: If I could answer that digression for a moment, with respect to our different understandings of respect, I was hopeful when I came here that after twenty weeks the Court would know my name.

In the end we came to love Bill and Len for what they were doing. By standing for the best and most neglected part of their tradition they were almost as heavily attacked as we were. After the trial, Bill was almost a client himself; he was blamed for crossing state lines to incite a riot in Santa Barbara. And Lennie was speaking at rallies too. If the Nixon-Agnew strategy is to frighten the "permissive" liberals away from the younger people, these two men were creating the only effective counterstrategy: *solidarity.*

So the story of our contempt is not unlike that of our defiance in the streets of Chicago the year before: people of different politics and life styles driven toward a common resistance. We did not know what would happen when we entered the streets, and we knew just as little when we stepped into that courtroom to see Julius Hoffman sitting under the Great Seal of the United States. There was no conspiracy, no preplanned design. If the government is looking for the cause of the confrontation, it will have to look beyond the courtroom to the raging conflicts in America that no legal structure can contain.

IX

The Jury

It was an American verdict.
— SPIRO T. AGNEW

The trial had to come to some kind of conclusion just to prove that it works. It hurts people but it works. And it's everybody's responsibility to make it work. I think it shows that American society as a whole can be made to work.
— JUROR KAY RICHARDS

Going upstairs to the jury room on the first day of the trial, we felt like the early Christians being paraded before the Romans. Under the cold neon glare sat several hundred people who looked collectively like a Republican state convention. It was the silent majority making a rare public appearance. They are silent because they have no grievances that require expression in the streets, since they can express their grievances by convicting radicals. There was hardly a black or a young person in the room. No hippies, not even what you could call a young "mod."

We tried unsuccessfully to challenge the procedure by which our jury was being selected. The jury panel foreclosed any chance for a trial by our peers. It did not even represent a real cross-section of the community. The voter lists, from which juries are selected, systematically exclude racial minorities, the young, the mobile, and those who are alienated from the American political process. We, the critics of the political system, were to be judged by people who were registered in it.

We were worried too that the FBI or the police had in some way directly manipulated the process. Jessica Mitford's book on the Spock trial revealed that the registrar had artfully excluded women from the baby doctor's jury panel and that the FBI had run a security check on each of the 5000 panel members. Veteran Chicago trial observers also gave us the impression that our panel was older and whiter than those usually found in the Federal Building. In answer to our questions about FBI checks on this jury panel, Foran merely scoffed.

But as the trial continued we came to feel the presence of police influence on the jury more clearly. First, a week later, suspicious letters stating "We are watching you—The Black Panthers" were sent to two jurors, one of whom was Kristi King, who seemed as though she might be sympathetic because she was young and had a sister in VISTA. Such letters are totally contrary to Panther policy, and the term "The Black Panthers" has never been used in party communications. Kristi's father apparently brought the letter to the attention of the FBI. The judge called her into court, showed her the letter for the first time, and asked if she could continue as a fair and impartial juror. Shaken and without time to think, she replied, "No." The other juror, who turned out to be an enemy, already knew about the letter and had discussed it with her roommate and told the judge she thought it was her "duty" to continue serving.

Second, we opposed sequestering the jury, and when our motion was denied, we opposed the U. S. marshals' acting as jury caretakers unless we could supply defense staff to play the same role. The marshals acted as disciplinarians for the judge in court, keeping us quiet, arresting and beating spectators, just "neutrally keeping the peace" in the face of our "provocation." These same marshals were the courteous and selfless guardians of the jury for five months, getting to know them personally, arranging for their entertainment and comfort. While we were attacking the credibility of police agents in court, they showed all of the James Bond movies to the jury at night. They were part of the police apparatus we were attacking, yet they were the only party to the trial with direct contact with the defense, the prosecution, the judge, the jury, and the outside world.

At the beginning we also requested the privilege of questioning the prospective jurors about their attitudes toward racism and the Panthers, the war and the draft, the generation gap, and long hair. This *voir dire* procedure is allowed in some lower courts, but federal rules gave Judge Hoffman discretionary power over the procedure. He was satisfied to ask the jurors their names, addresses, occupations, and whether, if selected, they could be fair. Even this shallow questioning revealed that a large number of those whose names were called had family or social connections with the police. Through our challenges we removed the ones with overt ties, but there was no knowing the real backgrounds of those who remained.

Picking the twelve jurors and two alternates is a form of gambling. A name is called; you watch the possible judge of your fate walk to the jury box; you scan the face and clothing, try to catch a vibration or two, listen to the tone of voice as he answers the simple questions. The government goes first with its challenges. If it accepts the twelve sitting in the jury box, we must either make a challenge or accept the twelve as the final jury.

We chose to play this rigged game; it was an attitude we kept throughout the trial. Finding ourselves in a setting constructed by our enemies, we realized that the problem was not simply to expose it but to use it whenever possible without trapping ourselves. We felt this ambiguity not only toward the legal procedures but toward these "middle Amer-

ican" jurors most of all. Were people from such backgrounds
hopelessly brainwashed into hostility against us, or were they
capable of understanding the need for radical change? We
knew from experience that a silent minority of this "silent
majority" was against the war, against racism, and supportive of their kids' new life style. We knew that only a few were
needed to hang a jury.

So we played. We guessed that the prosecution was waiting
for us to exhaust all our challenges, then accept the jury
under a protest that we were being deprived of a fair choice.
Having fewer challenges, their tactic was to hold until we
were out, then knock off every juror who appeared in the
least bit open to our case. A few potentially good ones appeared, including a black electrician and a college student,
but they were knocked off peremptorily by the government.
A few other possibilities remained in the jury box, middle-
aged folk looking as if they could be spoken to. One in particular caught our attention because she was carrying a book
by James Baldwin under her arm as she walked to the jury
box. She was Jean Fritz, a Des Plaines housewife on whom
great hopes would eventually rest and great pressures would
fall. Another was Kristi King, the girl who was tricked off the
jury a few days later. We decided: accept the jury as it is, before we lose the few friends we might have. We stopped, and
we could see a look of upset surprise on Foran's face.

Our strategy was to achieve at least a hung jury. Such a result would badly damage the government's morale by showing that the people are an unreliable agency of repression.
Though never staking our faith in the jury, we had reasons
for hope. Mrs. Fritz's daughter, in a frightening display of innocence during the trial, popped up in a public meeting and
told Rennie not to worry, because her mother did not believe
the government had proven its case. A few days later, we
sweated through a government investigation of the daughter's statement, and we exulted when the government did not
move for Mrs. Fritz's final dismissal from the jury. There

were little things too, like facial expressions, that convinced us we had a chance.

But our strategy depended on civil disobedience on the part of friendly jurors. They would have to think of themselves as the highest authority in the courtroom, a role virtually forbidden them by Judge Hoffman, though honored more than once in earlier American history. They would have to reject the appeal to national security, see through the lies of police witnesses, stand up to social pressures of all kinds, and refuse to compromise their principles. In the end our greatest fear proved to be true: under pressure, even those who knew we were innocent could not hold out.

The scene during the jury-selection process set the tone for the trial. What a scene it must have been: eight madmen in bright clothes passing notes, climbing over the table, whispering, laughing, arguing over the appearance of the jurors. We were judging them, putting them down, shaking our heads, looking sharply at them, yet *we* were the ones on trial. The pattern was set. They would have the power, but we would not be weak and suppliant: we would dominate the courtroom. This heresy would not be lost on the jury. It would come to constitute possibly our greatest crime—disrespect.

"I was a streetcar conductor. I've seen guys, real bums with no soul, just a body—but when they went in front of a judge, they had their hats off. These defendants wouldn't even stand up when the judge walked in. *When there's no more respect, we might as well give up on the United States.*"

That was the impartial philosophy expressed after the trial by the jury foreman, Edward Kratzke, whose wife welcomed him home from sequestration with oxtail soup and a new color television set. Mrs. Ruth Peterson, the juror who said it was her "duty" to be impartial after receiving the threatening letter, later said we had "no respect for [our] elders." As an example, she pointed out that we put our feet on the government's furniture.

A remarkable story of the jury's deliberation was copyrighted and published immediately after the trial by the youngest juror, Kay Richards, who proclaimed herself the negotiator of the final verdict. According to her story, two of the twelve thought we should have been shot, eight believed we were guilty, four felt we were innocent. If Kristi King had remained on the jury, according to Kay, she would have been a fifth sympathizer.

Even though she convicted Abbie, Kay wrote, she wanted to meet him and read his books. She felt the trial began to liberate her from a prison of social isolation. A computer operator from tiny Escanaba, Michigan, she knew no blacks and recalled that her whole life "was revolving around the money I could make; it was all computer, computer, computer." Despite her "straight" appearance, during the trial some defendants thought she was giving us sympathetic looks—but, she confessed, it was only to make us feel that we were being judged as "human beings." However, the split verdict, which she engineered, sounded more like it came from Kay's computer than from her humanity.

This verdict was hailed by liberals and conservatives alike, by the press, and by Foran and Schultz as a vindication of the judicial system. Because the twelve jurors reached a divided verdict, it was assumed that they had not been "taken in" by either side, that they had exercised a discriminating common sense. But the only common sense was the jury's decision to acquit everyone on the conspiracy charge and to acquit Lee and John on both counts. This was a common sense that could not understand the abstract legal definition of conspiracy, that assumed a conspiracy meant a tightly knit group of people making secret plans together, and that recognized vast differences among the eight defendants on trial. And it was a common sense that concluded that the government had no case on Lee and John in comparison with the others.

Otherwise, the jury deliberations revealed all the absurdity of the legal system in fine detail.

First, *the jury assumed our guilt rather than our innocence.* They took the government's case at face value, not understanding it as a combination of fantasy and fabrication, and expected us to rebut each moronic charge in minute detail. One juror, for example, believed it was "suspicious" that we were not at the big scenes of violence during Convention Week—as if we had known where the police would make their attacks. Our attempt to discredit the police mentality and to present an altogether different reality was not convincing to a jury which believed that we must have done something wrong if we were indicted and brought to trial.

Second, *the jury did not debate or understand the facts.* The jury kept arguing "those big issues," such as permits and police brutality. They could not recall the details of speeches or alleged acts, and the judge refused their requests for a rereading of parts of the transcript. "We had heard five months of testimony, with note-taking forbidden, and now we just couldn't remember it all: we weren't sure who had said what. . . ." Even before the jury went out to deliberate, they were divided not over facts but over their fear or approval of our life style, which they discussed indirectly in arguments over how to raise their children. Kay even wrote that our appearance (the way we looked at the jury) intimidated some jurors into sympathy with the police.

Third, *the verdicts were unrelated to the crimes charged.* "We couldn't understand the indictment. We didn't really know what the charges were." The two defendants charged with concrete acts, John and Lee, were acquitted. The rest of us were found guilty of provocative speeches in Chicago. Jerry and Abbie, according to Kay, "went beyond mockery." Dave and I used ambiguous and "irresponsible" language. But however incendiary these speeches were, they had nothing to do with the question of our *intent* in crossing state lines before we arrived in the police-state environment of Chicago, and *intent* was the crime charged in the indictment.

Fourth, *they compromised on punishment, not on their understanding of the facts.* "A compromise on punishment" were Kay's own words. She negotiated between the two deadlocked groups of seven and four. Instead of sitting around a table arguing, then arriving at a common agreement about the case, they reached their verdict more in the manner of a labor-management settlement. The two groups of jurors did not even sit in the same room during part of their deliberations. According to Kay, one of the jurors "thought there should be severe punishment." Two others "hated to give up the maximum sentence." But in the end they compromised because, according to Ruth Peterson, "half a chicken is better than none." Kay wrote that she alone was happy with the verdict. In other words, eleven people delivered a verdict that none of them individually believed conformed to the facts.

It was not so much our enemies on the jury who concerned us as it was our friends, the four women who apparently thought we were innocent. In Kay's account, these women believed that the law was unconstitutional, and this became Kay's negotiating wedge. "I argued that was for an appeals court to decide; it was our job to decide if the law had been broken, nothing else." Others have told us that the social pressures on Jean Fritz, for example, became unbearable, mentally and physically; the insults and innuendos challenging her patriotism and her sanity finally took effect.

The jury *twice* sent notes to Judge Hoffman claiming they were hopelessly deadlocked. The Judge never even answered the notes, leaving the impression that a verdict was imperative.

What caused both sides to compromise was an overwhelming loyalty to the system. Foran's final words in summation

—"Do your duty"—seemed to Kay "an impossible task; it meant that this jury must reach a verdict." A hung jury would symbolize the failure of citizens to perform in the expected way, a further sign of the spreading disorder. (Kay again: "If we have to have laws, somebody has to support them and enforce them.")

The moment they walked into the courtroom with their verdict we knew from the drawn faces of our friends that they hadn't been able to hold out. And as the verdicts were read, it all fell into place; the crazy indictment itself made sense: two counts for each defendant, with Weiner and Froines thrown in with the "big six" so the jury would have plenty to bargain over.

We often ask, why did the German people permit the rise of Hitler? The answer was in the defeated eyes of our friends. They had come a long way—through many years of conservative suburban life, through a system that instructed them to believe and obey authority, through a male-dominated society that made them select a man as the foreman of a jury of ten women, through countless subtle pressures during the five months of trial—and now they were sickened, and perhaps ruined emotionally. The marshals proved to be the key rationalizing force for the jurors with doubts, as Kay's description of the final scene shows:

"A matron named Ruth was standing in the doorway when we got back to the jury room, and she said: 'Don't be that way. Don't take it that way. *You did what you had to do.*' And we went into the room and we all broke down. Ron Dobrowski, the marshal in charge of the jury, came in and said: '*I don't see what else you could have done.* My heart goes out to you. . . .' "

There was something hopeful in the fact that, after all, four of twelve members of the silent majority believed us. But four of twelve in the Gallup polls believe in unilateral withdrawal from Vietnam as well. They are willing enough to register their opinions but too defeated to live them.

Fascism will come to America by compromise: not through the strength of reaction but through the weakness of the good people.

If that is the tragedy of the older generation in America, it is not yet that of the young. Even as we were sentenced, Rennie pointed out that "our jury is in the streets."

The Trial
in Perspective

X

Justice in the Streets

The conspiracy trial in Chicago seemed to bring the whole scene into focus. It would be hard to overstress the fascination felt by students here for the events in Judge Hoffman's courtroom. They became topics of daily conversation.

—RICHARD FLACKS AND MILTON MANKOFF

"Revolt in Santa Barbara: Why They Burned the Bank"
(*The Nation,* March 23, 1970)

The trial was a reliving of the 1960s. Chicago was not the only focus of testimony. The significance of other landmarks was also recounted: Selma, Berkeley, Columbia, the Pentagon, People's Park. Our witnesses recalled our history. Mark Lane and Dick Gregory charged the CIA with political assassinations; Tim Leary (later jailed himself) and Allen Ginsberg relived the be-ins; Cora Weiss read a letter from a survivor of Song My; Julian Bond described the violence of the South and the funeral of Martin Luther King. The testimony traced our gradual development as revolutionaries: Bobby, a comedian, GI, mechanic, community worker, then a Panther; Rennie, a chicken judger, basketball star, student-government leader, SDS founder, community organizer and peace activist; Abbie, a graduate psychology student, civil-rights worker in the North and South, organizer of a peace candidate's campaign, then a dropout on the Lower East Side—six of us who came alive in the Beat Generation, former graduate students, civil-rights workers, peace marchers, and campaign workers. We had been building a movement for ten years. Now it seemed that all of that movement was on trial. And we were the scapegoats.

This feeling was confirmed when we spoke around the country, meeting thousands of young people who felt themselves to be part of the ordeal. They read about the trial in the underground and overground press; it was a grotesque theater in which the whole country seemed to be the cast. First it was comedy, featuring Judge Magoo. Then with the gagging of Bobby it became tragedy, and Hoffman became Hitler. It seemed endless, a nightmare without awakening, a horror show without intermission.

We felt the solidarity of young people every day inside the courtroom itself. Despite the freezing Chicago winter, thousands of anonymous young people wanted to attend the trial. To get one of the fifty or sixty available seats each day, they had to line up outside at about five or six in the morning. During Abbie's and Daley's testimonies, they were wrapping themselves in blankets at midnight. Ceaselessly harassed, they were treated worse than we were. Chicago has a 10:30 P.M. curfew for kids, so one morning at six o'clock ten of them were arrested for being "too young." The lucky few allowed by marshals to enter the building were met by new ordeals. Everyone was searched, made to throw his coat and possessions on the floor in the hallway, and ordered not to smile or whisper or to make any noise while in the courtroom. If the spectators had to leave for any reason, they were subject to losing their seats. Often they were forced to leave when they broke the rules by gasping or laughing. For these "crimes," many of them were beaten. The thudding of fists and the screams of pain became part of the pattern of insanity. We sat helplessly; the press took notes on the "disorder"; Bill would describe it for the record; and the judge explained that keeping order was not his responsibility, but that of the marshals.

The press was shocked by the violence of The Day After only because it had failed to cover the presentation of our case to the real jury of our peers. During the course of the trial we spoke in public perhaps 500 times. During the November Moratorium alone we appeared and spoke before a million or more people. At small schools where we spoke, often more than seventy-five percent of the student body turned out. These were not "lectures"; they were political events. We addressed the audiences as our jury and asked for their support, considering their standing ovations to be demonstrations that would be heard in Washington. We said that our trial, unlike any other, provided an opportunity for a collective offensive by our generation against Nixon, Agnew, and the Justice Department. It was true: the audience was part of the Conspiracy, all with a real stake in turning back repression. They knew it and they felt it.

We were not leaders in command of legions of youth; we were a myth in which millions could participate. We were symbols of what millions were going through themselves. It was not a one-way flow of energy between the Conspiracy and its supporters. We were moved and shaped by the collective rising anger of these thousands of others.

Outrage over the trial was translated into violence no less than three times nationally: in the October Days of Rage; at the Washington Moratorium in November; and on The Day After. Previously, most radical violence had been in defense against swinging clubs. But on these three occasions people were fighting back against blows coming down in the courtroom. The only "organized" violence came from the Weathermen in September and October.

Rulers first fantasize their devils, then create them. We never did what the government accused us of in 1968, but the Weathermen did in 1969. What we did in 1968 prefigured Weathermen: a few karate and snake-dance exercises, some disruption, a lot of running in the streets, and at the end of Convention Week a prediction that a fighting force would be created that would bring the war in Vietnam home. It remained for the government to develop this seed into a paranoid image of crazy, unruly, drug-ruined, club-carrying, communist-inspired mobs rampaging in the Loop, and for Weathermen to fulfill the image one year later. Many Weathermen leaders were shaped by the events of Chicago 1968. When our legal protest was clubbed down, they became outlaws. When our pitiful attempts at peaceful confrontation were overwhelmed, they adopted the tactic of offensive guerrilla violence. When our protest against the war failed, they decided to bring the war home.

And so, even as we were sitting in court, the new revolutionaries conspired to come to Chicago to "incite, organize, and promote a riot." Though there were only 200 Weathermen, the Days of Rage resulted in the destruction of a famous statue of a Chicago policeman, shattered windows in the Loop and along the Gold Coast, injuries to police, and a broken neck for the same corporation counsel who had moved with the front of our own marches the year before without mishap.

John, Abbie, and I went up to Lincoln Park the opening night of the Weathermen war. They looked exactly like the people we were accused of being: helmeted, wearing heavy jackets, carrying clubs and NLF flags, they stood around a fire of park benches exactly like a primitive, neophyte, nervous army. They asked us to say a few words of greeting. It seemed like an invitation to another indictment, but we agreed. When I got up to speak, however, Abbie and John thought better of it and disappeared. I said a few words praising the spirit of their new militancy, looked around nervously at the photographers taking pictures of me with the bullhorn, and got out of there. It was the first army I had ever addressed and speech-making seemed out of place. An hour later we learned they were for real, even if they had small numbers. What they told us would be a "demonstration" near Judge Hoffman's ritzy Drake Towers turned out to be a literal rampage.

After the four-day Weathermen action, the press besieged us for a statement. They wanted one that could be boiled down to either praise or condemnation. But we were not going to condemn in public any group that was escalating the struggle, so we issued a statement emphasizing differences but condemning the hypocrisy of those who ranted about Weathermen violence while ignoring the violence of the American empire. In the statement we concluded, "America reaps what she sows."

Several of us had deeply mixed feelings about the October action. We were drawn to the seriousness of the Weathermen, for here at last was a group willing to go beyond the pseudo-radicalism of the white left into a head-on showdown with the system. The New Left was rapidly becoming the Old Left, a comfortable left, with too many radicals falling into the ruts of teaching and monogamy, leaving Che and Malcolm and Huey only as posters on their walls.

But there was something deeply wrong with what had happened in Chicago. At first we could only understand the symptoms. Smashing car windows, for example, was not "materially aiding the Vietnamese"; it was just plain random violence. And only 200 or 300 people had come to the Weathermen action, instead of the thousands the Weathermen had promised. To us revolution was like birth: blood is inevitable, but the purpose of the act is to create life, not to glorify blood. Yet to the Weathermen bloodshed as such was "great." They were striking terror into Pig Amerika by breaking windows, and their tiny numbers would be unimportant, they claimed, in the vast myth they were creating.

During the Moratorium a few weeks later, several thousand people streamed toward the South Vietnamese Embassy one night, then toward the Justice Department the next day. They too were violent, but their targets were more selective and meaningful than those of the Weathermen in Chicago.

Abbie wrote that the difference was between structured, artificial violence (Weathermen) and natural, spontaneous violence (Yippie). The Weathermen believed in "war," chose an arbitrary date, and then just began it. But most young people could not relate to scheduling a riot, partly because of the debatable effectiveness of such a tactic, but mainly because it was not a spontaneous reaction to an immediate situation. Weathermen violence was dictated not so much by a situation as by an ideology. Their violence was structured and artificial, because in their heads they were part of the Third World. They were alienated from their own roots. The privileged, funky, hedonistic qualities of youth culture turned them off. The cultural revolution among youth was to them simply more pig privilege. They were not guerrillas swimming like fish among the people; they were more like commandos, fifth columnists, operating behind enemy lines. Eventually, this logic would lead to their glorification of the media image of Charlie Manson—a cool, totally alienated killer—as perhaps the best "model" for white youth. They were not the conscience of their generation, but more like its id.

We felt, on the other hand, that there was a genuine, legitimate revolutionary consciousness arising out of the life experience of young people. We were not simply allies to a revolution centered in the Third World. As the misfits of a dying capitalism, we were oppressed in unique ways and had to rebel in unique ways. Our revolution would be part of an international revolution, to be sure, but with its own style and content. Our will to struggle would come not simply from the inspiration of the Vietnamese or the blacks but from the imperative of preserving and expanding our own way of life.

There are limits, however, to any notions of spontaneous rebellion. Abbie's criticism of the Weathermen relied too much on the alternative of spontaneously "doing our thing." In the face of repression it becomes irresponsible and hazardous simply to propose that people go wild in the streets. A workable organizational machinery becomes necessary to push the struggle at all levels, including in the streets. In a sense the Yippies used Washington to push for militancy. Though they had a base of support in the crowd, they lacked machinery. They were exploiting an event put together by others; the only people who were organized in Washington were the peace-movement moderates.

We learned how organization and spontaneity could go together on TDA (The Day After). We had *leadership* (the Conspiracy), *machinery* (the network of campuses where we spoke, the underground press, and so on), *strategy* (massive protest by "our jury" as a reply to Justice Department intimidation) and *flexible tactics* (people were told to invent their own actions but to make them both militant and broadly based). If it was true that this was "our generation on trial," no more organization would be needed.

That is why, on TDA, there was a riot across state lines that shook the country. Young people who had not come to Chicago to "bring the war home" were striking back now, for a purpose they believed in, with a spontaneity flowing from legitimate outrage because their collective identity had been violated and they could stand it no longer. Weathermen had created the tactics, but the fight was around our own needs.

Tens of thousands participated. The youth ghetto in Santa Barbara exploded and the Bank of America was burned down. Stores were trashed everywhere. Bombs were placed in buildings from California to New York. The trial, which had been designed to intimidate, had produced insurrection instead.

We didn't "organize" it; we only called for our jury to reach its verdict in the streets. It erupted spontaneously. In Berkeley the crowd wouldn't even wait for the speakers to finish denouncing the trial. The form it took confirmed that more than eight were on trial. People riot when they themselves feel that they have been slammed against a wall.

We eight were representative people, acting out many of the impulses of our generation. It was like riding the crest of a great wave, a wave made by the power of the people.

XI

Thoughts on Political Trials

Officials charge that we are disrupting democratic institutions in order to create chaos and, later, revolution. In fact, by our existence we expose the unreality of democratic claims. By acting as if basic rights belong to all Americans, we expose the fact that in reality those rights belong only to a few. Our assertion of an equal humanity creates our strategy: we find that America cannot be both an empire and a democracy. The American empire requires vast outlays of money and military personnel to protect investments and power interests. As the backbone of the free world, America is led into support for a network of unpopular reactionary regimes. Given the growth of social revolution as an ineradicable fact of modern times, America must become more of a military state, taxing and drafting its own people and consequently stifling any real aspirations at home. Democratic institutions become more hollow in the process and "Power to the People" becomes a revolutionary slogan.

We brought the same attitudes and strategy from the streets into the courtroom.

The court in American society is something like the church. There is a widespread conspiracy to hold the court holy, above the world of sin and deals and power. It is to be treated with a special respect; quiet is to be observed by those who enter, and speech is only to follow formal procedure. The judge is a high priest possessed of a wisdom that mere citizens do not have. He wears robes, makes interpretations of obscure scriptures, and holds a gavel (like the cross) representing authority. He is referred to as "Your Honor" or "If the Court please . . . ," much as the Pope is "His Holiness." Perhaps more than any other public institution in America, the court system demands an absolute conformity to its rules and its atmosphere. If citizens will only respect this institution, then all their conflicts can be sifted, negotiated, and resolved.

At the same time, everyone knows that this concept of the courts is a myth. The court is political; the judges are elected or (in most cases) appointed by politicians. Behind those robes are men of political motivation: landlords, underworld figures, partisan manipulators. Nearly all of them are white, middle-class, middle-aged, conservative males. The laws they administer favor rich against poor, white against black, respectable against nonconformist.

When the courts are turned into a weapon against change, trials must be turned into an attack on the courts. Treating a trial politically means dealing with the courtroom the way it *is,* not the way it is ritualized.

Our trial represented an opportunity to test and expand these principles on a national level in full view of a wide audience. Some of the understanding we gained in the five trial months can be reduced to these general guidelines:

1. *We are political prisoners, not criminals.* Never permit the government to reduce the case to the ordinary dimensions of a criminal trial; make it known that American citizens are being jailed for their political attitudes or, in our case, for their "state of mind" by a state that cannot reconcile its pledge of a fair trial with its stake in preserving the status quo.

2. *The people are the jury.* The scene of a political trial should extend into the final courtroom of public opinion: never let the judge and prosecutor muffle the proceedings

from the public under any guise. Unlike ordinary criminal trials, a political trial should be tried in the media. Through speeches, rallies, and demonstrations, we have to carry our defense to the public. In this way we take the legal camouflage off repression and expose it for what it is. We create a sympathetic climate of opinion that the government must either placate or alienate. We exercise political influence on the higher courts. If we are acquitted by a jury of the people, then the government becomes the criminal, even if we are in jail.

3. *Our politics must be carried into the courtroom.* We cannot resist illegitimate authority in the streets only to bow politely before it in the courtroom. We have to make clear in court that it is our identity, our politics, and our life style that the government is attacking. We have to appeal to the jury, outside and inside the court, to accept our politics as legitimate. Without risking needless time in jail, we must risk "contempt of court" when the court is brazenly in contempt of our rights. We should experiment with acting as our own lawyers as a way to place our identity directly before the jury and the larger public.

4. *Internationalize the issue of repression.* Alert public opinion throughout the world to the fact that the United States is cracking down on those who want peace, racial solidarity, and self-determination. This causes growing embarrassment for American public-relations men, creates strains in our relationships with "allies," especially in Western Europe, and encourages the struggle of those who are fighting imperialism on their own soil. The government must recognize that the road to domestic repression is the road to its own isolation as an international outlaw nation.

5. *Battle even within the system.* Recognize that a jury, no matter how unrepresentative, is not totally under government control. Further recognize that since the government is not completely monolithic, an appeals court might reverse a conviction, depending on the political climate and the legal rec-

ord you have made in your case. Involve competent lawyers in the defense, if only as "advisers" if you defend yourselves. Propose reforms in trial procedure that, if accepted, would make political persecution more difficult or, if rejected, would still educate the public to the existence of alternatives.

6. *Do not fear repression.* Social change involves sacrifice and pain. Jail cannot always be avoided. Punishment is the ultimate weapon used to control dissent. While not courting punishment, do not fear it. If you conduct your defense properly, the repression will be exposed and the people educated. In jail you can organize prisoners to serve as a symbol or conscience for people on the outside and can help to make the existence of political prisoners a real issue.

7. *Use the trial to advance the general goals for which you were indicted.* Legal repression is used to place the entire Movement on the defensive by tying it up in court costs and explanations of past actions. Repression deflects energy from the basic programs of ending the war and racism. But if the trial is used to attack vested interests, it can become a new front of struggle for the general Movement. At the same time that the judiciary is being confronted in the courtroom, defendants should show that they have not been knocked to the sidelines, by continuing to participate in demonstrations and political activities outside the trial.

These principles constitute a way to fight a rigged system while avoiding being trapped "inside" (dependent on the grace of the system) or isolated "outside" (unable to take full advantage of openings and contradictions within the system). The goal is to make the government fall into a political dilemma: if it moves repressively, it tarnishes the image of justice. But if it relaxes the repression, the dissenters it seeks to control are released back into the community. The underlying belief must be one of faith in the power of the people, not the power of "enlightened" authorities. A mobilized public is the only source of power to force concessions or, failing that, to replace an illegitimate government.

Anyone who feels our principles are too extreme might be surprised to find them being rejected as too moderate by victims of oppression in the near future. Since our trial, several people—blacks like Rap Brown, clergymen like the Berrigans, white radicals like the Weathermen—have decided that it is preferable to go underground rather than accept trials and imprisonment. On a less visible level, thousands of young people arrested for dope or protest are evading the law rather than showing up for punishment. We are entering a time when dissidents are being treated more like prisoners of war than like political heretics. In these conditions, a campaign to free all captured prisoners will become more important in the years ahead than strategies limited to trial defense.

XII

"You People Have

No Alternatives"

The trial shook the judiciary. Like mayors, university presidents, and generals before them, the legal authorities began a frenzied campaign—not to reform their system but to defend order against this new threat. Judges called for the jailing of dissident lawyers. Counterinsurgency projects were begun in law schools and bar associations. At the University of Michigan Law School, for instance, the Ford Foundation funds research on plastic booths in which to isolate disruptive defendants. Attorney Louis Nizer believes that these booths will not prevent defendants from "grimacing" and suggests that "unruly defendants be jailed, and then provided with daily minutes of the trial and be allowed to follow the proceedings on radio and television." The gagging and shackling of black people is evidently embarrassing to the modern state; plastic compartments or video tapes are more suited to our "advanced" civilization. All these measures, of course, will have to respect the rights of the defendants to a fair trial, say the authorities.

These proposals for law and order in the courtroom will have no more effect than have the new gadgets acquired by police departments across the country after ghetto rebellions. Efforts to protect "order" not only expose order as fascism but make the system less secure and less stable. The spectacle of political trials being conducted with prisoners in plastic bubbles would do even more than our trial to convince people that the law is tyranny. Defendants themselves might well decide to go underground rather than be kept like animals in these modern cages.

Those who look forward to greater repression of course cannot conceive that there are alternatives. But what is amazing is that with all the panic over courtroom disruption there is almost no one within the system willing to suggest reform, instead of a tightening of repression.

One alternative to preserve order within the system would be to stop all political indictments, jailings, bond refusals, and trials. This alternative has been suggested by Jessica Mitford in her book on the Spock trial. As our trial has demonstrated, a commitment to "get" the political heretic can lead only to an intensification of the rigging of the legal process. No fair trial is possible when politics is the crime. The government sets up confrontations that discredit its own courts in its attempt to punish and coerce dissenters.

Such a policy change need not at first alter the basic class and racial injustices that are built into our courts and our prisons. It would merely respect the right to militant organization among those people trying to change the system. It would attempt to defeat radicalism through mobilizing public opinion in a contest of ideologies, instead of by courtroom persecutions.

What would be abandoned under this alternative would be the policy of repression. The anti-riot law would not be passed or, if it was already on the books, not enforced. President Nixon would instruct John Mitchell to seek no conspiracy and draft indictments and to dismantle the task forces pursuing the Black Panther Party. Non-religious objectors to the Vietnam war would be honored; a tacit amnesty policy would exist for exiles to Canada; and private negotiations would begin for the safe return of Eldridge Cleaver.

This policy would regard the First Amendment as an instrument of transition, a bridge to the future rather than a bridge to be burned. It would aim at preserving the democratic right to organize above any other immediate interests of the state. Its antidote to "anarchism" would be the preservation of the right to assemble peacefully. If these rights are as effective as the state claims, those who try to go outside them would be isolated within their own community.

With or without this policy change, there is a second way to avoid "violence in the courts": *through basic procedural reforms.* Instead of imposing the ridiculous façade of "judicial neutrality" on a situation that is never neutral, it is possible for the courts to be open to a fairer and fuller explanation of political issues. Instead of an adversary system, which rewards the most accomplished casuist, why not a system committed to the fullest exploration of the facts?

Three obvious reforms, for example, would have made our defense easier to wage. First, the selection of the grand jury and the jury should have been conducted on a more representative basis. The court should have dropped all procedures discriminating against minorities, youths, and political dissidents in the formation of a jury panel. Second, the rules of evidence should have been opened to permit discussion of all vital political information concerning Chicago 1968. The court should have allowed a full discussion of the intent, philosophy, and background of all parties to the conflict. Books, films, and articles, as well as expert testimony, should have been permitted so that a verdict could have been reached based on a total understanding of the confrontation. Third, our jury should have been free to participate fully and significantly in the trial process. They should have had the right to nullify the judge's rulings and to pass judgment on the law itself. Permission should have been given for the opposing attorneys to argue the merit of the law before them. Question-

and-answer periods, or some form of full discussion between ourselves and the jury or between the jurors and any witnesses they would have liked to have called, should have been allowed.

One could continue to list almost indefinitely such proposed reforms. But they are not suggested in any hope that the government will be listening. Nor are they suggested as ammunition for liberal arguments. They are intended, rather, to demonstrate that the problem is not one of finding alternatives but one of finding power. These are all fully legal alternatives and all of them would improve the system and lessen violence in the courtrooms—but they will not be implemented because they do not serve power. Such reforms would threaten lawyers, judges, politicians, and all those with a vested interest in preventing the people from becoming more informed and more aggressively engaged in dealing with the issues of the time. Instead of exploring reforms, our political rulers have sent Warren Burger to the U. S. Supreme Court and Bobby Seale to a trial in which he might be sentenced to the electric chair. These are not policies aimed at "restoring order"; they are policies aimed at creating violence in reaction to dissent. *The result will be a new generation of outlaws.*

XIII

The Limits of the Conspiracy

The Stones are STARS—on tour if not elsewhere, automatically the center of attention and privilege. None insists on that status, but they accept its security with an equanimity both innocent and arrogant. . . . The Stones, and certainly Jagger, are the tour's essential promise, and therefore, if not always right, never wrong.

All non-Stones are relatively insecure and in a constant struggle to maintain their own egos, and their own place, in the graded orbits around the Stones. While on the one hand there is an undercurrent of hostility to the Stones—why do they always get the dope first?—there is a stronger one of self-dramatization, a pressure to maximize one's importance to the Stones. That, in turn, increases the Stones' status, and everyone is more important if the Stones are more important.

—MICHAEL LYDON
"The Rolling Stones—At Play in the Apocalypse"
(*Ramparts,* March 1970)

Too many people looked up to us, regarded us as a rock group, wanted posters and the Word. There were many good people who came to work on the trial with the hope that it would be a communal project with fantastic individual possibilities; but our personalities, and the structure of the trial itself, did not allow that. The truth is that although we served an important revolutionary purpose for six months, we discovered a lot that was wrong about ourselves. Even though our identity was on trial, even though our habits were truly radical compared to those of bourgeois society, that hardly meant that our identity and habits were revolutionary by our own standards. In different ways we all came to sense our own limitations.

Most of these limits stemmed from the fact that the seven of us are white middle-class males, accustomed to power and status in the Movement. The Youth International Party, all myth aside, is run by two persons, Jerry and Abbie. The National Mobilization, in its prime, existed as a coalition that revolved around Dave Dellinger. Rennie has functioned time and again as the brilliant director of an office-centered organizing project, and I have always been more of an independent catalyst than an equal member of any collective or group. Bill and Lenny too are accustomed to having a bevy of women and others working for them in a service capacity. We were not good about sharing power, rather than competing for it, among ourselves. We were even worse about sharing power with the hard-working staff that chose to labor in our shadow. Like any other business, the Conspiracy organization pigeonholed people into roles. Bob Lamb handled press relations; Dottie Palombo handled our financial affairs; Linda Miner handled all negotiations for films; Sue Burns took care of the transcript; Stuart Ball and Micki Leaner handled legal research and preparations; and so on.

All of them did the grimy work that kept the Conspiracy rolling. They even purchased our airplane tickets and had them ready for us as we streaked out of the courtroom to keep our speaking engagements. The Conspiracy as a whole never consulted with any of these people about fundamental trial strategy, and their growth as whole people was hardly allowed in the situation. We were particularly oppressive to women; most of us, though proclaiming to be part of the liberated culture, were involved in all-too-traditional relationships with the women in our lives. The women on the Conspiracy staff—below the wives in order of rank—were nearly suffocated as a result.

Even if we had been able and willing to improve these relationships, the structure of the trial made it difficult, perhaps impossible. None of us had ever been required to appear on time every morning for six months anywhere—much less at a trial in which we were worked over for seven hours a day. The trial necessitated discipline—we had to produce our witnesses, our motions, and our bodies—or else. This crowded out time for democratic decision-making or the nonexploitative relationships we are supposed to be building. In addition, our staff and friends had to deal with more than the usual intimidation in the presence of our powerful personalities. We were the center of the drama because our lives were at stake, they felt, which made it even more difficult to raise criticisms or questions about the direction the trial was taking.

For the few of us who worked on the defense, these pressures were incredible. It was an eighteen-hour day: worrying about the next stage of testimony, settling disputes with other defendants, calling and readying witnesses, worrying about their travel difficulties, getting our trial lawyers prepared to take the witnesses through their questioning, fighting with the mass media to obtain cameramen and films. The situation required arbitrary and often instantaneous decisions. When the other defendants asked me to "coordinate" this work, I had no idea it would be the worst organizational ordeal of my life.

Working within that structure of trial discipline made me into a high-pressure machine. It seemed necessary to push aside anyone who could not work efficiently and compatibly, and it was impossible to tolerate hang-ups, identity problems, or even demands for a full discussion of what we were doing. My personal relationships shriveled to nothing in Chicago. I compartmentalized my personal life, left it in Berkeley, and went there whenever possible on exhausting overnight flights. I would drop a pill on Monday morning to turn on the production machine again. It always seemed necessary, for a revolution is not a be-in; it requires periods of discipline and painful work.

Our male chauvinism, elitism, and egoism were merely symptoms of the original problem—the Movement did not choose us to be its symbols; the press and government did. The entire process by which known leaders become known is almost fatally corrupting. Only males with driving egos have been able to "rise" in the Movement or the rock culture and be accepted by the media and dealt with seriously by the Establishment. (There are a few isolated women who as exceptions prove the rule: Bernadine Dohrn and Bernadette Devlin are seen as revolutionary sex objects, Janis Joplin and Grace Slick as musical ones, Joan Baez and Judy Collins as "beautiful and pure.")

The first step in this power syndrome is to become a "personality." You begin to monopolize contacts and contracts. You begin making $1000 per speech. With few real friends and no real organization, you become dependent on the mass media and travel in orbit only with similar "stars."

The media's interest in Yippies—whose image dominated the trial—illustrates this process frighteningly. Random House not only publishes *Woodstock Nation;* it takes part in the put-on with a cover illustration in which its trademark building is shown being blown up. Simon and Schuster is pleased to advertise Jerry's book, with his approval, as "a Molotov cocktail in your very hands," "the *Communist Manifesto* of our era," and "comparable to Che Guevara's *Guerrilla Warfare.*" Who is using whom? Publishing a book with revolutionary content is certainly possible under capitalism, but what does it mean when a corporation joins in an advertising put-on about the destruction of its own system? It could mean only that the corporate executives and advertisers sense something familiar and manageable in this revolution. In Jerry's book especially, what must seem familiar is the marketing of a personality. The book consists mainly of interesting episodes from Jerry's life. Jerry becomes the Important Person as his history of the Movement unfolds; other people disappear. Women are unmentioned (although a photo of his wife Nancy's smiling face bobs across two full pages of Quentin Fiore's "medium-is-the-massage" layout). The content is in contradiction with its own Yippie philosophy. Ideally leadership is supposed to be shared, or even to be "nonleadership," but here it is embarrassingly self-centered, deliberately and consciously marketed.

There is much of value in this book, just as there is in the music of the Rolling Stones. But there is finally something unreal. For the Rolling Stones, "street-fighting" is a lyric, not a reality that they support or participate in themselves. The irony will be if Jerry—or any of us, since we all are like him in one way or another—ends up like the Stones and other rock celebrities. In the Yippie world, toy guns are carried around for media effect and books are the only Molotov cocktails. But will they really "do it"? If not, then the theater of personality finally will become acceptable to the weird appetite of American culture. Impossible? At the trial's end, we were seriously planning to sell movie rights to big commercial producers, and Abbie (whose *Revolution for the Hell of It* was sold to MGM) was declaring, "Let them have Washington, D. C.; we're going to take over Hollywood."

During and after the trial, we argued over the future of the Conspiracy. Differences emerged around whether we should become a permanent leadership group in the Movement. The Yippies wanted a kind of American Apple Corporation: Conspiracy books, posters, records, sweatshirts, and so on. They and Rennie wanted the Conspiracy to be a kind of institutionalized high command of the revolution, leading national campaigns and building a local organizational structure. The Conspiracy had the popular base, the moral authority, and the fund-raising capability, they argued, to become a major outpost of radical opposition just at a time when other organizations were folding or fragmenting. Not to do this was to cop out on a rare opportunity.

We were all in agreement on the priority of organizing around the Connecticut, New York, and Chicago trials of Bobby Seale and other Panthers, and of campaigning against the Justice Department's repression of black revolutionaries. We were in agreement too on the necessity of continuing education about the issues of our trial during the appeal. And we would speak to raise money wherever local people were facing political trials without support.

In my view, to go further—toward becoming a high command—would be forgetting our limits and perpetuating our worst tendencies. We are just the kind of individualists around whom a movement should not be consolidated. We are valuable perhaps as a resource to draw upon, but not as a leadership to unite behind. Our power interests and our male chauvinism would be a drag on the growth of revolutionary energy.

In addition, we had no common politics. We were united against repression, but not united *for* anything in particular. Dave is hardly a native of Woodstock Nation, Rennie is hardly into revolution "for the hell of it," and as Abbie himself testified, "we couldn't agree on lunch." The Conspiracy was only a compound of two outmoded organizations: the Mobilization and the Yippies. The program of periodic national mobilizations demanding a Vietnam policy change has certainly reached a point of uselessness, and the Mobe has shown no capacity since Chicago to create continuous local resistance or more militant tactics. Since the Chicago Convention it has become more and more a bureaucracy, older and more moderate than its base of young anti-war militants. The Yippies are also victims of legitimacy; their "cultural revolution" has become respectable since Woodstock. The politics of dope, sex, and spontaneous expression, while still persecuted, is also more and more able to find protection behind liberal opinion. The edge of the cultural revolution that has not been co-opted is moving beyond Yippie theater into the concrete areas of local organizing, self-defense, and drastic changes in the relationships between men and women. Mobe and Yippie can be seen as forms suitable for creating issues in the sixties that must be solved in the seventies by a movement that combines cultural revolution and internationalism, goes from symbolic protest to deeper levels of struggle, and replaces media leaders with collective leadership forms.

We are, after all, products of the sixties. The styles and forms of that time were perhaps as necessary as they were problematic. In a white movement that arose from the nothingness of the fifties, it was no accident that leadership went to articulate, aggressive males, and no doubt this pattern will continue for some time. But forms die, or at least change, and the test of a revolutionary may be how well he or she adapts to new possibilities. Among these possibilities are the growth of a radical feminism that is justifiably enraged at male political power, and the appearance of new, younger radicals (both men and women) like the Weathermen and White Panthers whose political attitudes stem from a much deeper alienation than what we experienced in the early sixties. From women comes the insight that our power is "male" in character; it is a power that involves conquering and subduing others, as opposed to a power that is collective and respectful of people. From the younger revolutionaries in general comes the insight that our pressure politics, our peace mobilizations, and our theatrics, though legitimate in raising issues in the sixties, are inadequate to the task of surviving and making revolutionary changes in the seventies.

To continue as revolutionaries we will have to abandon the old forms and become part of the new possibilities. One of the most revolutionary decisions possible is for leadership to refuse to consolidate its own power and to choose instead to follow new vanguards. Only by making such a decision will the conspirators be relevant to the future.

From Resistance
to Liberation

XIV

The Eighth Conspirator Is a Prisoner of War

(I)

Bobby Seale, like other Panthers now in jail, is not a political prisoner. He is a prisoner of war.

While the white Conspiracy defendants were at least able to speak, write, and freely prepare their defense, Bobby was seized on the Berkeley streets, indicted on a Connecticut murder charge, secretly driven in chains to Chicago, denied his right to representation, chained again, gagged, and severed from the case, shipped back to California and then off to Connecticut, where he now faces the electric chair.

If ours was the "political trial of the century," Bobby's long trial is becoming the definitive trial of black people in America. His facing the electric chair is symbolic of black people facing genocide.

Bobby's case is not unique. Nearly thirty Panthers have been killed since the party was founded; in the first year of the Nixon administration, over 400 were arrested on various charges; Panther offices in Los Angeles, Oakland, Chicago, Des Moines, and fifteen other cities have been attacked by police. Nearly all members of their original Central Committee have been suppressed: killed, jailed, or forced into exile.

The Justice Department has a special task force on the Panthers; the FBI considers them the greatest single threat to our national security; at least two congressional committees and several grand juries are investigating them.

The Panthers are the target not of repression but of an undeclared war. Under a state of repression, the heretic at least is accorded bail, trial, and appeal. In a state of war, victims are killed or rounded up without serious regard for legal "niceties." The Panthers held in jails across America today are no different from prisoners held in Santo Domingo, Saigon, or any other center of the American empire.

(II)

The escalation of war against the Panthers has created a vast difference between them and their less oppressed allies. The Panthers correctly criticize whites for not moving rapidly enough to deal with the special repression inflicted on blacks. And the whites, hesitant and confused about how to react to the brutal repression of Panthers, are correctly critical of the broadside nature of occasional Panther attacks on student movements, women's liberation and the cultural rebellion arising from conditions in the Mother Country.

These differences cannot be understood without a perspective on the history of black-white political relations. In 1966 black radicals, led by Stokely Carmichael, purged whites from the "integrated" civil-rights movement and directed them to go into the white community. Young whites did just this, creating a rebellious consciousness inside the Mother Country. Eldridge Cleaver and the Panthers then saw the possibilities of this white radical impulse and put forward a strategy of "liberation in the colony" coupled with "revolution in the Mother Country." The Panthers argued that blacks should wage an autonomous struggle for self-determination but added that victory would not be secured until the Mother Country was also transformed from within. They began to experiment with coalitions for specific purposes with white organizations.

Few whites realized the risks that the Panthers took in pursuing this line. It left the party exposed to constant, baiting criticism by black "cultural-nationalist" groups that preferred either no contact with whites or, if necessary, contact with white foundations and corporations rather than white radicals. Among black radicals, the Panthers were raising fears of a return to old-style coalitions, in which black people had been submerged and their interests made secondary to the class struggle. From great numbers of blacks, including those who joined the party, the Panthers were demanding an incredible psychological adjustment: to conduct a racial struggle without anti-white feelings. White radicals, by comparison, had very little to lose from the coalitions.

Since 1967 one coalition after another between the Panthers and whites has been created, achieved something useful, then been more or less dissolved as a result of racial or political differences. Some have been mainly educational campaigns, like the relatively successful one waged around Huey's trial. Some have been abortively electoral, like that made with the Peace and Freedom Party, which collapsed before the 1968 elections. The Panthers have searched for the most effective white allies and have come up with different answers from time to time. Sometimes the answer has been the broad liberal community and the students; sometimes poor whites in Chicago and Richmond; sometimes Yippies and street people; sometimes the peace movement; sometimes a mixture of two or more of these. Always the coalitions have been affected by the fact that the Panthers are far more revolutionary and serious than their allies; always they have been plagued by the question of whether whites should be considered essentially as "supporters" or as an independent radical force moving toward a front-line alliance with the blacks.

(III)

All these problems came to a boiling point in 1969 as Nixon's policy of repression escalated. In response to severe attacks, the Panthers proposed the formation of a broad United Front that would serve essentially as a support group. The Front would raise funds, educate white people to the dangers of fascism, and help circulate a petition for "community control of the police."

The difficulty was that the liberals who would be most likely to join such a front were having jitters about the Panthers and repression, and the younger radicals were going through the birth pains of new struggles. In the white community it was the ineffectual and opportunist Old Left groups that were most interested in the United Front. The radicals, meanwhile, were moving in at least four different directions: toward white working-class organizing, women's liberation, the cultural revolution (as asserted in the People's Park struggle), and armed struggle (as embodied by the Weathermen). Few of the younger radicals wanted to join a United Front with the Old Left or circulate petitions in the white community, and none wanted to accept Panther leadership.

Perhaps the Panthers did not understand the devastating effect this United Front would have on the young whites. Since their inception the Panthers had gradually inspired significant numbers of whites to the idea of armed struggle. Few whites had become John Browns, but the Panthers' heroic image was accelerating white revolutionary consciousness as no American movement had done before. Then, with little preparation, the Panthers suddenly adopted a reformist tactic that the whites had been trying to go beyond. White radicals had no objection to a United Front of middle-class liberal support for the Panthers. But they wanted the Panthers to recognize as well the need for militant liberation struggles in the Mother Country.

To the Panthers, the response of white radicals seemed self-centered and "anarchist." The embattled Panthers had difficulty understanding the priority of women's issues, for instance, or the significance of drugs and rock and roll, or why the Berkeley radicals fought in the streets for seventeen

days when black people had already demonstrated the futil-
ity of riots, or why Weathermen wanted to pick up guns instead of petitions. They could not see the legitimacy of the
struggles that whites were engaged in and began to assert
that the party should be the "vanguard" of the Mother Country as well as of the colony. The result was much hostile and
futile "commandism" from the Panthers and much alienation among the whites.

Before the cleavages could be overcome, the U. S. government moved to take advantage of the situation. Noting that
the United Front conference had ended in disarray and division, it concluded that the Panthers were isolated and therefore easy targets.

From the United Front conference through the trial these
gaps between the Panthers and their white allies continued.
In San Francisco on November 15 David Hilliard was booed
by the liberal peace movement for suggesting that peace
could not be achieved without a liberation struggle, and that
Nixon (or anyone standing in the way of black liberation)
should be killed. Seeing the black-white division, the power
structure moved again, this time indicting Hilliard for
"threatening the President."

During the trial the gulf was both narrowed and widened.
We enjoyed a political closeness with Bobby Seale, yet he remained in jail every day, while we were free. We helped
create a mass consciousness among whites about the repression of the Panthers, but Bobby was the one who experienced
the gagging. We asserted our unity with the Panthers but
could do nothing to prevent Bobby's sentence and the mur-
ders of Fred Hampton and Mark Clark. The inadequacy was
not simply our own; it existed throughout the white Movement. Until November 15 in Washington, not one major
demonstration occurred to protest what had happened to
Bobby.

Early this year, the Panthers were beginning to reconsider
their basic strategy of coalition. Eldridge drafted a manifesto

declaring that if class struggle were not possible, then blacks should go it alone in a race war. The manifesto vowed that no more Panthers would be sacrificed on the "altar of inter-racial harmony."

Then, suddenly, a hopeful new coalition was being created in New Haven. It had taken a long time (the Panthers had been held in Connecticut dungeons since before the United Front conference), but whites were beginning to move again on the issue of racism. A strike began in April. The president of Yale granted the validity of the issue the Panthers had been raising all along: that a fair trial for black revolutionaries in America was hard to imagine. When 25,000 people, called by the Panthers and the Conspiracy, came to New Haven on May Day despite the warnings of Spiro Agnew and the threat of the National Guard, a militant United Front involving both moderate and revolutionary whites at last began to appear.

(IV)

To understand the unevenness of black-white coalitions is to understand the structure of racism. All whites are part of a racist system: they live better materially, never experience the daily crises that the Panthers do, never are repressed as severely as blacks. Even becoming "more militant" than blacks cannot erase the color line: whites who try to act like John Brown are usually seen by blacks as manipulators who will not have to bear the consequences for whatever repression they bring down. The racial barrier that holds whites above blacks does not mean that all whites are individually racist in their attitudes or that white support is unimportant. But the attitudes, including alienation and protest, that develop in the Mother Country are remote from and often contradictory to black feelings. Women's liberation will tend to seem secondary to Panthers fighting for physical survival; hippie life styles will seem indulgent to blacks looking for work.

Huey Newton pointed out these differences in an essay from prison on white "anarchists." Huey wrote that the black community, experiencing collective oppression and collective material needs, will grasp the idea of organization and discipline much more quickly than will the young alienated white person whose goal is self-expression. Breaking out of slavery requires a personal change in black people far different from the new life style of young whites. The black is moving from dependence and powerlessness to an aggressive pride in collective power. The young white is breaking out of the straitjacket of conformity toward a sense of personal experiment and discovery. The young white will view organization and discipline as an infringement on free consciousness.

The white radical plays a difficult part in this ambiguous world. The radical professes solidarity with the Panthers and the ghetto. At the same time, as a white the radical receives special privileges and as a Mother-Country radical, experiences special needs for liberation that are quite different from those that move the black community. The white radical is thus likely to exemplify both the nearness of and the difficulty of achieving real solidarity. In political terms this means that although whites can help the black struggle, they are inherently undependable. While blacks will never have to "go it alone" completely, the principle of self-reliance is more basic than that of coalition.

A comparison with the coalition strategies of other national liberation movements shows parallels as well as vast differences with the American situation. Both the Vietnamese and the Algerians dealt with a French left that contained racism and national chauvinism. Yet while they fought, the Algerians—and especially the Vietnamese—patiently educated and organized the French people because they knew that French public opinion would be needed to support an end to the war. In the current war also the Vietnamese have taken a patient attitude toward American public opinion, believing that the war would encourage dissent and a new political atmosphere in the United States. Their strategy is to conduct a long guerrilla war, waiting for the cost in blood, taxes, and honor to awaken some Americans while tiring others. While a "revolution in the Mother Country" would be desirable, they believe mere *divisions* are enough to bog down the United States. Beneath this strategy lies a remarkable faith in the ability of human beings to overcome ignorance and prejudice. The Vietnamese believe that even the American soldiers they are fighting are pawns who would change sides if they knew the truth. The moral force of an idea is their greatest weapon. They are not a "vanguard" giving commands to the American anti-war movement but more of an armed conscience trying to move and persuade.

But in the American case the black and Third World colonies are dispersed *inside* the Mother Country. There is no national territory on which blacks can develop schools, industry, and agriculture, establish an identity as a people, and fight for their freedom. A war of independence here would not end in the political separation of two distinct geographic territories, as it did for France and Algeria; it would rearrange America itself.

One result is that black people in America have become more interdependent with white people than in any other colonial society. Feelings of both familiarity and hatred are bred at the same time. Although they are culturally separate, blacks can think like white Americans easily and naturally. The hypocrisy of even the white radicals is felt day to day.

Painful relations can often be broken off, but this one has a way of continuing. Even while blacks despair of whites, black motion itself constantly pushes some whites toward a better, more radical understanding. Blacks have been the trigger of the early white student movement, the radicalizers of the anti-war movement, the legitimizers of revolutionary violence, and the soul of the underground culture. The black assault on white racism has its effect: young white people become less racist than their elders even though they remain part of a racist system.

The black-white relationship becomes hard to break for another reason. Because they lack a unified national territory of their own, blacks are almost forced to depend on a "base" in the consciousness of the white left, or on the bank accounts of white liberals—more so than in other liberation struggles. In Vietnam the revolutionaries can leave political relationships with the Americans to skilled and patient diplomats. They are confident that their image of the American people will be fulfilled, but they do not go through the psychological torment of dealing with whites every day. They shoot those who invade; they welcome those who protest. They do not need immediate evidence to confirm their ultimate faith that whites can be human beings; they gain strength enough from their schools, their factories, their army, the land they till, and their national tradition. In America none of this seems possible, at least not in the form taken by other peoples. As long as there are no "Panther zones" as fully self-sustaining as the "Vietcong zones," the black-liberation struggle will be tormented by its dependency on the support of the white left.

So white radicals are in a coalition with the black struggle —even if the coalition is not recognized formally—simply because we are part of a common dialectic. In the case of the Panthers, we will either vindicate their gamble on white support or become evidence of white failure and therefore bolster "cultural-nationalist" arguments for years to come.

It is sufficient to understand and act on the fact that the black colony is a time bomb inside the fragile center of the colonial Mother Country. The eventual detonation of that bomb will wreck a system that dehumanizes all its people, and it will not leave our lives or social structure intact.

If we consider the issue in the framework of colonialism, we can see most clearly what must be done. We can see that the demand for black self-determination cannot be accommodated by a welfare state that is colonial in its power relations. We can see that the Vietcong started without white support, alienated most Americans, yet are winning their own struggle and contributing immeasurably to ours. We can see that the differences between white and black radicalism are not antagonistic, because our destinies are bound totally together.

(V)

If we consider the Panthers as embryonic Vietcong in the United States, if we assume that a Vietnamese situation is developing here, it becomes logical to adopt and improve the strategy of the anti-Vietnam war movement and direct it against the aggression at home.

First, *this would mean recognizing that Bobby Seale and other Panthers should not even be tried in the courts of the present U.S. government.* They go to trial only under protest. As prisoners of war, the Panthers should be freed not by higher courts but through negotiations coming about because of public pressure. The slogan "Free Huey" must be enlarged to "Free All Political Prisoners." Many whites cling to the concept of a "fair trial" for the Panthers because they do not want to accept fully the idea of self-determination for blacks. This leads them to believe that they should examine the "facts" of Panther court cases before deciding to support the Panthers. But even such a paternalistic approach would still vindicate the Panthers. In New Haven, for instance, it would reveal that the High Sheriff selected his personal barber and several other "friends and neighbors" for the grand jury that indicted the Panthers. It might even reveal a high-level government plot to frame Bobby and the others.

But the most enlightened approach that a white could adopt toward the "facts" would be to dismiss them as irrelevant, as an internal matter of the black colony. This is no different from the issue of "terror" by revolutionaries in Vietnam. All we need to know is that the Panthers, like the NLF, rely on popular support, not on coercion, for their success, and that the colonial invaders rely on massive terror to frighten away that popular support. If white Americans are concerned about the "terror" of the Panthers, they should stop police aggression in the ghetto instead of condemning black extremists at cocktail parties. Bobby was indicted not for his supposed role in a killing, but as an effective way to remove him from the streets and scare away support because of the gravity of the charges.

Second, *we need a nationwide "political education class" or "teach-in" as a tactic to create consciousness of this emerging domestic war.* It is curious that whites have spoken thousands of times in the Vietnam teach-ins, but have done so little to take the issue of the Panthers to the same audiences. The amount of continuing political education needed cannot be underestimated.

Third, *taking to the streets against racism and repression can be as important now as it was in the earlier phases of the anti-war Movement.* The recent strike and massive demonstration in New Haven was the first time that whites have come out in large numbers for the Panthers in a nationally visible way. The national student strike triggered by the Cambodian invasion would not have included the demand to free the Panthers were it not for the initiative of the New Haven strikers. The trial in Connecticut will continue to create an urgent climate in which effective demonstrations are possible. Plans should be made for demonstrations from now through the end of that infernal trial, with the definite objective of freeing the Panthers "by any means necessary." Where trials are not an immediate focus, the new Justice Department might well be. As a symbol of centralized evil, it can serve as a target institution the same way the Pentagon has for the anti-war Movement.

Fourth, *forcing a conflict within the national Establishment over this question is crucial in order that repression against the Panthers be slowed down.* Repression can be foiled in the short run only by creating sharp divisions among America's powerful elites. The anti-war campaigns of the Senate doves were crucial to slowing and sometimes preventing military escalation, and they gave respectability to dissent in general. There is, of course, the danger that such dissent will cool the militant edge of protest, but only in the unlikely event that the Panthers come to rely on the Establishment for their survival. If Ramsey Clark or Kingman Brewster wants to become the William Fulbright of our domestic Vietnam crisis, it will be to the benefit of the Panthers and everyone but the all-out racist aggressors.

Fifth, *we must initiate international campaigns to brand the United States as a criminal and outlaw government.* Probably the chief problem facing the American ruling class is not Vietnam, but the survival of the United States as a racist nation in the new international scene. American racism is the number one foreign policy problem for this country. Each step of racist aggression further isolates the United States in the world; each concession to the blacks for the sake of "national image" only raises the domestic confrontation to a higher level. Using all its international contacts, the American left should expose the repression of the Panthers in every conference and journal in the world.

Finally, *we must create a resistance structure.* There will have to be active, extra-legal cooperation between white and black revolutionaries on every front of the struggle. A new underground railroad to protect the fugitives and resources of the black colony may become a necessity. This need is likely to become especially real in America, where the black communities are geographically surrounded by whites and where communication and transportation are almost exclusively controlled by whites.

The trial of Bobby Seale and the Connecticut Panthers is the best possible point of departure for a new upsurge of white support for black liberation. The government is hoping that one bolt of electricity will kill the spirit in all of us. The gag and chains of Chicago were not enough; they are now being replaced by the electric chair. Every sane person has a stake in preventing this maneuver—and it *can* be prevented. Just as our case was turned into a trial of our generation, so Bobby's can be turned into a symbolic trial of black and white people in this country.

XV

The International Imperative:

All for Vietnam

The American plan, as envisaged by Tang, is first, the introduction of more troops into Vietnam; second, greater bombing; third, stationing soldiers along the Ho Chi Minh Trail, thus involving troops from Thailand and sealing off the Cambodian-Vietnamese border; fourth, expanded bombing of the Laotian Liberation Front forces; and finally, an attack on China. . . .

But, he granted, "even if worse comes to worst" and the war is escalated to China, "your movement will have failed, but we are prepared to suffer more."

> —from a January, 1966 interview with a
> Chinese official, in *The Other Side*, by
> STAUGHTON LYND AND TOM HAYDEN

The solidarity of the progressive world for the Vietnamese people has something of the bitter irony faced by the gladiators in the Roman Circus when they won the applause of the plebians.

> —CHE GUEVARA

American officials are considering the use of nuclear weapons on the people of Vietnam.

This possibility seemed no longer a paranoid fear but a

clear and present danger. As we arrived in New Haven for the Black Panthers' May Day Rally, the atmosphere of the town certainly made the worst seem possible. Staid and respectable New Haven had been transformed: it was dark and shuttered and under military occupation. Agnew had called for Brewster's resignation. Paranoia about a government engineered massacre was everywhere. In this setting we listened to Richard Nixon explain the escalation into Cambodia.

The crisis atmosphere of New Haven made the threat of a total American escalation finally believable, but the thought itself was not new. From the teach-ins we knew that John Foster Dulles proposed using the ultimate weapon to aid the French at Dienbienphu; in the Columbia student strike we came across "professors" who were consulting with Saigon officials on the use of tactical nuclear weapons; returning Vietnam veterans told of using launchers from which nuclear-tipped rockets could be fired; the "nuclear option" was considered during the siege of Khesanh; and we knew that Curtis LeMay's supposedly crackpot philosophy of "bombing them back to the Stone Age" was shared by such sophisticated persons as the military analyst of *The New York Times*.

Rennie, Dave, and I knew, above all, from the Vietnamese themselves who told us they were prepared to suffer two million deaths as a result.

We knew that our trial was part of a repression against those who had organized the Vietnam Day Committee, the Pentagon and Chicago confrontations, and the various trips by Americans to North Vietnam—a repression intended to pave the way for more escalation in Southeast Asia.

We were not alone in "thinking the unthinkable." The invasion, Kent State, and Nixon's Cold War rhetoric all caused a sudden panic among millions of Americans who yearned to believe in "Vietnamization" and other promises of peace in Southeast Asia. So great was the national reaction that it sent Nixon before television cameras and ulti-

mately to the Washington Monument to cool down the
threat of disruption in his own capital. Nixon's promise to
withdraw from Cambodia had a temporary cooling effect,
but it also blew away many a lingering illusion about peace
in Asia. The government had served notice to all but the
most blind that its intention was to win the war through escalation.

Why did anyone ever doubt it?
The U.S. government already had demonstrated its will-
ingness to attempt a subtle genocide in Vietnam under the
pretense of waging a "war of attrition."
The military ruthlessly bombed the social structure
(schools, hospitals, dams) of Vietnam, poisoned the rivers
and farmlands with chemicals, drove the rural population in
the South into concentration camps, and spoke of "destroying cities to save them," "fighting against the Vietnamese birth rate," and "threatening their existence as a nation."
The toll of suffering in Vietnam long ago surpassed that
which would result from a Hiroshima-type attack.
Genocide by any other name is still genocide. Perhaps the
original Americans who became involved in Vietnam only
believed they were helping the French regain domination;
later, that they were trying to create a "showcase" through
the Diem government; later still, that U.S. advisers could
"win the hearts and minds of the people," or that B-52 raids
would bring the other side to the negotiating table. Regardless of the intent of particular officials during the last 21 years
of American intervention, the dynamic is unmistakable:
there has been relentless American military action to crush
the Vietnamese revolution by any means necessary.
First the Americans tried to restore the French to power.
Then, after Dienbienphu, they refused to sign the Geneva
Accord but instead created SEATO and sent technical aid to
Diem. Then they sent military advisers and, when their puppet army began its final disintegration, American ground
troops and aerial bombardment. When forced for political

reasons to stop bombing North Vietnam, they expanded the war in Laos and intensified the bombing of South Vietnam.

Seen in this long perspective, Lon Nol is the Ngo Dinh Diem of Cambodia. It was American-trained Cambodian mercenaries who moved in from South Vietnam to establish the power base from which Sihanouk could be overthrown, and it has been those same mercenaries (along with those from South Vietnam) who are attempting today to slaughter Cambodian nationalists and Vietnamese residents of that country which for twenty years has remained at peace.

The invasion of Cambodia was more than an attempt to shore up the Lon Nol government, or attack NLF sanctuaries, or expand the war to weaken the reserves of the other side, or any of the other rationales offered after the fact. The invasion was designed to increase the American stake in Asia, at a time of mounting pressure for disengagement, by provoking the other side into an all-out confrontation. The political and military history of Dienbienphu reveals a clear parallel to recent events in Cambodia. In 1953 the French hawks were beset by a gold crisis and domestic protests against the war, were weakened in their capacity to defend other imperial interests, and were badly beseiged on the battlefield. Despite this crisis they still dispatched ten thousand troops hundreds of miles from their Hanoi base to the remote and easily encircled valley of Dienbienphu. There the hawks knew their troops would be tempting bait for the Vietminh. Indeed they were, and a perilous battle began which flashed daily in the French headlines. When the French troops were dangerously pinned down, the pressures for escalation increased rapidly, and top American officials were eager to send troops or bombers if only the British would agree to make the intervention seem "multilateral." Only the reluctance of British officials and American Congressional leaders prevented the escalation plan from being carried out.

In this perspective, it is interesting to speculate what would have happened if Cambodian and Vietnamese liberation forces had decided to *bog* down and encircle the Americans rolling straightway through their "sanctuaries" and onward into Cambodia. If the other side had accepted the bait, as they certainly were equipped to do militarily, then Nixon could have faced this nation with the "necessity" of rescuing our troops in Cambodia by escalating (with more troops in Cambodia, resumed bombing of North Vietnam, etc.)

These possibilities are even easier to imagine when we understand Richard Nixon and the "China Lobby" orientation he represents. Nixon was elected to Congress on an anticommunist pledge at the time of the Chinese Revolution (which marked the beginning of America's intense worry over the Vietnam "dominos") and became, in the words of one historian, the "most competent" member of the House Committee on Un-American Activities. He believes the threat of using nuclear weapons brought "peace" to Korea. At the time of Dienbienphu he publicly advocated sending American ground troops to Vietnam, and tried up to the beginning of the Geneva Conference to arrange an escalation that would sabotage the negotiations.

The same Nixon, as recently as 1965, made his fanatic views perfectly clear:

victory for the Vietcong . . . would mean ultimately the destruction of freedom of speech for all men for all time not only in Asia but in the United States as well.

The conflict could not be clearer or more total.

But there is a very human desire to recover from shock; to return to normalcy; to disbelieve that the worst nightmares can become reality. All these feelings operate among Americans who want peace, and it is precisely these feelings that Nixon seeks to manipulate. Feelings such as these quite likely moved people in the national protests against the Cambodian invasion, causing a relieved satisfaction with Nixon's agreement to "withdraw" in two months. If the New Haven weekend offered a glimpse of the apocalypse, the calm protest in Washington D.C. just one week later readjusted most people to the conventional world of anti-war protest.

Escalation always has been followed by apparent lulls in the war, by peace feelers, and by reassurances to public opinion. After Cambodia it was not the Nixon Administration that implemented this pacifying side of Vietnam strategy. It came from the liberal Establishment that Nixon and Agnew despise.

Much of the effort needed to keep young people from believing that the nightmare time had come, was performed by liberal politicians and college administrators. Though politically despised by Nixon and Agnew, their safety-valve role helped the Administration through the crisis.

On Yale's signal, college administrators adopted a sudden new tolerance, even cooperation, toward dissent on the campuses. Just as Yale was "reconstituted" for a weekend to accommodate the Panther protests, so did schools everywhere allow students and faculty to work against the war. On the political front, a score of Senators came forward with anti-war amendments and proposals for channeling student energies into fall electoral campaigns.

The underlying motive of the administrators and politicians in all this was certainly not withdrawal of troops from Vietnam or radical transformation of the war-oriented university. Their immediate concern was peace in the schools and peace between the generations. A perfect embodiment of this concern could be found in the figure of Cyrus Vance, a Yale trustee who was intimately involved in keeping his "alma mater" from being destroyed during the May Day protests. Vance of course previously represented the U.S. government in the Paris talks. Like Yale President Brewster (and Yale trustee John Lindsay, to cite another example), Vance by now preferred a retreat in Vietnam to save America's interests elsewhere, particularly at home.

These men knew quite well the level of discontent on the campuses. They knew that the school year's two peaceful and legitimate Moratoriums had only widened the generation gap. They knew that the Conspiracy Trial added greatly to the despair of the young with established institutions. Above all, they knew that since January the level of revolutionary violence in America had increased by a great leap. Demonstrators in large numbers were breaking windows and trashing buildings. Young guerrillas were burning and bombing hundreds of institutions like ROTC and draft boards. They knew, finally, that Yale would be leveled in any confrontation during May Day weekend, setting off perhaps hundreds of violent rebellions on less-guarded campuses. In their calculation it was time for a new policy: to allow for peaceful dissent within their institutions even at the risk of ruffling Establishment feathers and exciting Spiro T. Agnew.

This is not to dismiss all the protest energy in the national student strike as wasted or coopted. Overnight thousands of new activists went into motion. Nixon was forced to limit the timetable of his invasion. Shock at Kent State, Augusta, Jackson, and Cambodia probably increased the conviction of millions that the war was worthless.

Now that the strike is over, however, we can see its limits clearly. No colleges were permanently "reconstituted," no fundamental pressures were generated against the war machine, most of the activity dissipated into summer vacations, and most college administrations preserved their buildings from violence. By contrast, a bloodbath was initiated in Cambodia; 40,000 South Vietnamese troops remain there; and the United States is planning to bomb there as heavily as it does in Laos.

The sense of *déjà vu* was all too real. We went through an exactly analagous experience in 1967–68 leading up to the Chicago confrontation. Then the "lunatic fringe" were not guerrilla-bombers; they were burning draft cards, obstructing Dow recruiters, and storming Pentagon walls. Then, too, the Establishment's crisis-managers (McGeorge Bundy comes to mind) were urging a cutback in Vietnam to prevent a breakdown at home. Then as now the message to young America was: don't believe the radicals, work within the system, create a constructive alternative to nihilism, and remember you'll be crushed if you try to rebel. Then also the young people went to the Silent Majority, worked in the very guts of the electoral system, became Clean for Gene. Then came the bloody finish in Chicago. Senator McCarthy next went off to cover the World Series for *Life* magazine. The moderates won their demands—negotiations with the other side, an end to the bombing of North Vietnam—only to realize they were meaningless. The government had ended the anti-war movement under the pretext of ending the war.

Amazingly, within a year optimism bloomed again among the same liberal forces who were shattered in Chicago. A group of former McCarthy and Kennedy workers (and politicians even including Averill Harriman) formed a movement curiously called the Moratorium. Everyone hailed it as a respectable alternative to the kind of politics the Chicago Conspiracy represented (we had to fight their bureaucracy even to appear on stage in the Chicago Moratorium in October). Indeed, a million or so people were mobilized around rather humble slogans like "give peace a chance." The response to this upstanding respectable protest: Nixon declared he would be unaffected by their numbers, and Agnew branded the organizers "effete snobs."

Evidently the Agnew criticism contained some truth since the Moratorium organizers swiftly gave up their plans for an escalating month-by-month boycott and work stoppage, and instead closed the Moratorium to return to the more familiar environment of electoral politics. The Cambodian invasion came three weeks later.

The pattern of liberal failure by now is obvious. From the McCarthy campaign to the Moratorium to the present campus "reconstitution" movement, we have seen a moderate

Democratic Party-oriented program tried and frustrated again and again. The problem in this political strategy consistently has been an over-reliance on politicians and an under-reliance on popular pressure. This is not the way liberal strategists would argue their cause, of course. They would say the war can only be ended by respectable efforts within the mainstream of politics, and that disruptive protest only alienates the public and strengthens the hawks. But they cannot be blind to the fact that whatever leverage they have is precisely attributable to their offering a "safe" alternative to disruptive radicalism. For a better explanation of their politics we would have to conclude that they want to end the war but also save the system. They do not themselves follow the natural path of radicalization which many of their followers do. They remain instead a loyal opposition working within the electoral arena for changes not in the system but in its priorities.

The tragedy is that many young people who accept these notions of change are simply not confident of their own power. It is not that they want above all to stay within the system. It is that they are conditioned to believe that working outside the system is impossible. They are still blind to the source of their tremendous power—the power to make Nixon rush to the Washington Monument. That power does not reside in their electoral potential but in their potential to disrupt the vital institutions containing them (the universities), to break the link between generations, to threaten the future stability of the country. It was this threat that caused Brewster to "open" Yale and Nixon to pledge "withdrawal" from Cambodia. There is a constant tendency among the students and young people in general to disbelieve the reality of their own power, to continue believing that power is with their parents or the politicians. Instead they should consider the Vietnamese formula about American politicians: *if we are strong, even a Goldwater will withdraw; if we are weak, even a McCarthy will attack.*

The radicals have always been more correct about Vietnam than the liberal architects of protest. The goals of the radicals, once condemned by liberals as utopian, now are quite acceptable; for example, the demand for immediate withdrawal instead of negotiations. The radical strategy, of relying on people in the streets instead of in the ballot box, has also been more productive—at least up through 1968 when the radical strategy reached a peak of success which has been followed by a permanent impasse.

In the year 1968 we achieved the first clear setback in the American escalation strategy. It was the year of military defeat (the Tet offensive) and political catastrophe. Westmoreland, McNamara, and Johnson bowed out unceremoniously. Those who came to Chicago to protest were prophets without honor. We held to two convictions: that despite Johnson's retirement, despite the Paris talks, the U.S. aggression would continue; and that the anti-war movement should remain independently in the streets instead of placing itself at the disposal of "peace candidates." The Chicago confrontation was the peak of a year that demonstrated that any political leadership committed to staying in Vietnam would face domestic chaos and, ultimately, electoral defeat.

But at the same time we learned that in the face of chaos, "law and order" would be tried long before withdrawal from Vietnam. Moreover, from Johnson's abdication we realized that America's stake in Vietnam took precedence over the personal fortunes of whoever happened to be President. The costs we were imposing on the American Establishment were real but, at least for a while, acceptable.

And with that discovery, radicalism came to an impasse.

Up to that point, and even today, most peace activists and radicals believe that Vietnam is a flaw—a terrible flaw—in the working of the American Empire, which could be removed with a sufficient outcry of disagreement. Who would have believed that a supreme egomaniac like Lyndon Johnson would make winning the war more important than winning re-election? Who would have thought that with half the Senate and most of the press and public believing the war a "mistake," that it would nevertheless continue to expand?

There has been a widespread failure to recognize in Vietnam the most serious international showdown of our time.

Radical intellectual theories about Vietnam, for example, have assumed that U.S. involvement is irrational. Not irrational in the sense liberals assert when they blame faulty Presidential advisers for our Vietnam commitment, but irrational in the sense that Vietnam is not in the "true interests" of corporate capitalism. In the radical view, America is ruled by a flexible corporate elite with many interests throughout the world. In this empire Vietnam is a rather unimportant economic and political area (compared to India, Indonesia, Japan, Brazil). Since the corporate elite is concerned with the smooth overall maintenance of empire, and not with the occasional loss of a small domino, the radical reasoning goes, our powerful gentry will cut their losses in Vietnam and dig in better elsewhere. The United States can withdraw, says the intellectual, to Thailand and India-Indonesia, keeping a forward base against China while consolidating its grip on richer possessions.

This worldview provided most of the operating assumptions of the major anti-war groups in the late sixties—the Mobilization and the SDS—even though the two organizations were constantly at odds over strategy.

The Mobe did just what its name implied: it mobilized people to demand withdrawal from Vietnam. In most cases its demonstrations were large, legal, and peaceful, designed to allow a variety of people to surface their opposition to Vietnam. Between mass mobilization there were numerous attempts to do educational work among new constituencies, but local branches of the Mobe primarily existed to draw people to rallies. The presence of ever-larger numbers in the streets was effective in several ways: first, it helped individuals feel they were not alone in opposing the war; second, it gave politicians and influential figures confidence that they could oppose the war without being crucified, which in turn legitimized dissent among larger numbers of people; and third, it gave encouragement to the Vietnamese revolutionaries while demoralizing the American military and the puppets they supported.

But eventually the underlying assumption, that decision-makers would end the war if enough widespread pressure was created, was proven inadequate by the government's repeated escalation. While its structure remains, the Mobe direction has blurred, and support has waned since 1968.

The SDS radicals actually created the first national mobilization in the Spring of 1965, but then very quickly shunned a leadership role in the anti-war protests because they did not believe in the "pressure" strategy. Their radicalism, however, often led in perverse and sectarian directions. They assumed the anti-war mobilizations would be deceptively "successful" because the American Establishment, sensing a bad investment in Vietnam, would use the anti-war sentiment as a popular basis for pulling out. The peace movement would be coopted in the process, used by a new set of politicians (Robert Kennedy) for their rise to power. The real issue to SDS was not Vietnam, but the imperialist system that would continue beyond the withdrawal, a system that would strangle and threaten Vietnam (as the American blockade does to Cuba) and other nations until overthrown. In SDS language, there had to be an anti-imperialist movement able to muster resistance "seven wars from now."

In various local actions, SDS chapters made important anti-war contributions by their confrontations with recruiters and official spokesmen. But in the two major national confrontations against the war—the Pentagon and Chicago—SDS stayed aloof and hostile until the sheer heat of the conflict persuaded them to participate.

The SDS outlook was clearer than the liberal and humanitarian politics of most of the movement, but it was a terribly elitist view. Instead of regarding Vietnam as the crisis that would tear America apart and create conditions for domestic radicalism, a crisis that SDS should be deeply involved in resolving, they saw it more as an important issue for liberals.

There were other strands of radicalism—the life-style or cultural rebellions—which were even further removed from the issue of the war. Taking Vietnam as only a symptom of what was wrong with the country, many chose primarily to fight against their own oppression as longhairs. They opted totally out of the anti-war movement into what would become the Woodstock Nation. To the early Merry Pranksters as well as the later yippies, the anti-war activists were "straight" or "too political" or "on a death trip," not in touch with their own oppression and therefore no alternative to America. And so there developed a genuine alternative culture but its outlook, until quite recently, has been that of revolution-for-the-hell- of-it, revolution-for-ourselves "dope, rock'n'roll, and fucking in the streets" etc. Whatever impulse there has been against the war has had no outlet (except during Chicago) or has been channeled into a general rage against America.

The women's liberation movement, too, has been through a long alienation from the issues of Vietnam and the Third World. Rebelling against male-dominated structures in the anti-war movement, and focusing primarily on their particular oppression, they have assumed that the problem of Vietnam would be solved by others. Even during our trial, which was aimed at the anti-war movement, we could not generate a new level of interest in Vietnam. We spoke constantly of "the repression of the anti-war movement." We observed the moratorium inside the courtroom. We sent Bill Kunstler to Paris to receive news of American prisoners held in North Vietnam. Yet Yippie tactics made the news, and what aroused people the most was the naked form that Judge Hoffman's repression took. The very people whose nerves were deadened to the massive atrocity in Vietnam could be aroused by the relatively trivial oppression of the courtroom. Paradoxically, the Vietnamese knew better than anyone that the trial was about the future of the anti-war struggle. Throughout Vietnam ordinary citizens were concerned about our fate, and when we were jailed after the trial, our release was demanded by the other side in the Paris talks. How could the Nixon Administration speak of peace, they asked, while repressing the Chicago conspiracy.

Given the vacuum of militant anti-war leadership, it was predictable that a group like Weathermen would re-assert a revolutionary interest in Third World struggles. And the vacuum may also explain the extreme one-sidedness with which they would assert their politics. Against the view that emphasized the stability and flexibility of imperialism, the Weathermen began with the view that the Vietnamese and other Third World peoples are winning, that imperialism was in its death throes. They advanced a fifth-column strategy, although cloaked in a hippie life style and invoking Dylan as well as Regis Debray and Lin Piao. Their vision: "The pump don't work cause the vandals stole the handle." The exclusive task of white radicals, in their view, is irregular warfare behind enemy lines, inside American imperialism's fragile structure. Irregular rather than conventional guerrilla warfare because the Weathermen are doubtful of ever achieving broad popular support inside the United States. They assumed 80 percent of the American people are beyond redemption and seriously debated whether little children should be classified as "pigs." They are essentially agents, or John Browns, for the Third World revolution with the goal of materially weakening imperialism by over-extending its resources.

The immense contribution of the Weathermen has been in the assertion of internationalism and in their commitment to give their lives, rather than lip service, in solidarity with Third World people. But the problem in the vandalism or fifth-column strategy is that it fails to embrace the legitimacy of other struggles against oppression: women's liberation, cultural revolution, and so forth. Thus the Weathermen create a basic rupture between themselves and their natural base for revolution. The intertwined problem is that the Weathermen are underground by choice and necessity, thus cutting them off from any open leadership role in mass struggles against the war. They do not carry out the basic Vietnamese teaching that legal demonstrations, even activity by the liberal wing of the Establishment, can be more important to mobilize on certain occasions than a guerrilla attack.

•

So: the liberal anti-war movement has been trapped by its electoral strategy, the radical strategy is at an impasse, other revolutionaries have abandoned Vietnam to make their own oppression primary, and a few people have gone underground. Meanwhile, we are coming to the crossroads: either the Vietnamese people will win or be maimed horribly in a larger war. We will either stop the war or live under an intolerable barbarism.

Our task: an all-out siege of the war machine. Our watchword: All for Vietnam.

First and foremost, we need an Emergency Consciousness about the real danger of further escalation. The only way the Vietnamese, the Cambodians, and Laotians can secure their national rights is if the U.S. government is prevented from enlarging the war to include China and the use of advanced chemical or nuclear weapons. We cannot rely on liberal politicians to initiate this alert. At most we can include them in a united front, but the strongest Emergency must be sounded from the campuses like the University of California where the bombs are being processed, by the scientists who know what is going on, by the local anti-war groups outside military institutions, and by all revolutionary groups who are supposedly defending the Vietnamese Revolution. By forcing the government to answer in advance whether it is planning an ultimate genocidal blow, we can develop an international alarm which will make such an escalation far more difficult. We will also be laying the foundation for renewed militancy at home, since no tactics are too extreme in the face of this threat.

Second, Vietnam has once more to become a leading priority for all groups struggling to change the country. It cannot be assigned to an anti-war movement that is no more than a bureaucratic skeleton which goes into motion several times annually. The practice of organizing *only* around one's particular oppression is a self-indulgence in the face of the threat to Vietnam. It is also illogical because there are no Vietnamese inside this country; therefore, we have to speak for them. (The new interest in Vietnam by Yippie-cultural revolutionaries is a positive step toward internationalism that more organizations should follow.)

Third, the Vietnam war should be linked always with the issues of racism and repression at home. There still are many people, from the hardworking Trotskyists to the liberal opportunists who prefer to keep the issue of Vietnam "separate" for the purpose of drawing the greatest popular support. This political line is self-defeating for at least two reasons. First, it depresses and holds back the swiftly growing consciousness of hundreds of thousands of people who long ago were awakened to the war issue. Second, it neglects the obvious repression of the anti-war radicals and blacks who are being crushed precisely because they are causing difficulties for imperialism. If the Administration can gun down and silence Panthers, one might ask, why would that Administration have to worry about an unarmed and less together peace movement?

Fourth, it is time for the core of the anti-war movement to intensify the struggle with the goal of "cutting the supply lines" that feed the war machine. It is all well and good to make "reaching larger numbers of people" the goal of organizing, but there comes a time when time is running out, when there can be no more waiting for the Silent Majority or the Working Class to be taking the stand we have to take. It is time to ask what has become of the hundreds of thousands of people mobilized in the past for orthodox demonstrations, who are never called upon to do more than repeat performances. Is our "lack of numbers" and "isolation" the problem, or is it the cynicism and defeatism of those who have given up on stopping the machine?

The image of "cutting the supply lines" is meant to deflect focus away from politicians and toward the precious institutions that must run smoothly to carry out the war. Now is the time to cripple the machinery of war by a "siege of the Pentagon" from one end of the country to the other. The revolt of black GIs—and many whites as well—is a prime example of how to do it. Delegitimizing and shutting down ROTC which supplies the junior officers is another example. Preventing nuclear and chemical warfare research is another. We need to besiege corporations doing Vietnam business, to strike at the authority of every important individual and agency involved in Vietnam, to expose and identify the Vietnam Lobby as a group of War Criminals, to isolate, weaken, and stop their murderous program.

This siege strategy embraces the "mobilization and "guerrilla" tactics. The immediate problem is not whether tactics are too moderate or too militant. The problem is to recommit the energies of every sincere person for a last stand on Vietnam. The problem is to make people see that Vietnam is not a permanent part of the American way of life, but that it is a war with a dynamic leading to a showdown. By focusing on the issue of nuclear escalation and by identifying the Vietnam Lobby as the enemy, we can create the sense of urgency and the basis for broad support. By a siege of the Vietnam Lobby we aid the Vietnamese by making the war effort more difficult and costly.

One of the best ways to gain strength for the struggle is to explore and measure the contribution of the Vietnamese people to ourselves and the rest of the world's people.

The only way to drive out our cynicism is to realize that we are not alone and isolated inside the United States. We should follow the war not as a "tragedy" but as a struggle in which the side of humanity is making a stand so heroic that it should shatter the hardest cynicism.

Developing this sense of internationalism means going beyond the conceptions of Vietnam offered by the dove professors in the teach-ins. Their view, accepted widely in the anti-war movement, is that Vietnam is a case of "civil war" in which the Americans should not have intervened. The notion of "civil war" suggests that there are several Vietnamese sides with different ethnic and religious and political backgrounds, all quarreling among themselves. The implication is that Vietnam always has had internal problems which should not be very important to the U.S. government. There is no basis for solidarity with Vietnam in this view, only a basis for paternalistic regret.

This kind of thinking hides from people a history which is both educational and stirring. What has happened in Vietnam is no more a "civil war" than the American Revolution was a "civil war." The fact that some Vietnamese have identified first with the French and now with the Americans is no more significant than the fact that some American colonists were linked to the British.

The real history of Vietnam is a history of successful revolution which the Western powers have been trying to erase for 25 years. The important fact about Ho Chi Minh's 1945 Proclamation of Independence is not that he quoted the American Declaration (which the doves constantly use to show how cooperation would have been possible with him), but that he declared the independence of his country. The new revolutionary government was established throughout the whole of Vietnam. The basic conflict since that time has not been between Vietnamese. The Diem government, and the Thieu-Ky government were established by the United States and would fall without the United States; they have no significant roots among the Vietnamese people. The basic conflict is between the Vietnamese nation and American imperialism.

This Vietnamese nation is a threat to not only American generals but American professors and liberals, because of the revolutionary example it is establishing. The Vietnamese defy the military assumption that weapons can preserve America's power, and in their defiance revive a romantic revolutionary spirit that is supposed to be out of style.

In Vietnam the word "individualism" does not exist. The Vietnamese word that comes closest to individualism is "cannibalism." Their culture and their oppression have helped them approach the communist ideal, suffering, sharing, and struggling together. In order to survive they have had to become brothers and sisters in everything *before* achieving the technology and abundance that is supposed to make a socialist life style possible.

Their age-old fight against foreign aggression makes struggle seem to be in their blood. Their existence, like that of Cuba and Korea, demonstrates not only that socialist and national-liberation struggles can be joined, but goes further: they demonstrate that the Modern Imperial Colossus can be fought and beaten by a small country with primitive technology.

The Vietnamese people have fired the modern "shots heard round the world." They are defeating the United States in war, destroying the myth of American superiority.

In this triumph they have raised the spirit of millions of Third World people.

They have provided the triggering issue for the new student movements in Western Europe.

They have inspired black and brown people, and young white people, inside the United States itself.

More than any other people, they have come to represent the conscience of humanity. When Ho Chi Minh died he was the most revered statesman in the world.

And they have done it alone. The initiative has been theirs. They began fighting and dying long before there was a peace movement in America. They fought despite the fact that their communist allies were impossibly divided.

If it seems embarrassing or fuzzy-headed to mention these truths in America, it is because our country is an emotional wasteland too decadent to believe in being born again.

But if these truths continue to inspire greater numbers of Americans, the Vietnamese people will have to be thanked for a final gift: opening our eyes to our own history as a genocidal nation, and starting us on the road to our own revolution.

XVI

The New American Revolution

We for ten years incessantly and ineffectually besieged the throne
as supplicants; we reasoned, we remonstrated with Parliament in
the most mild and decent language. . . .
> —THE CONTINENTAL CONGRESS, "The Declaration of
> the Causes and Necessity of Taking Up Arms"
> (July 1775)

I feel that I am a citizen of the American dream, and that the revolutionary struggle of which I am a part is a struggle against the
American nightmare. . . .
> —ELDRIDGE CLEAVER

In the sixties we made our way
to the modern throne through trails of spilled blood. Now the
Nixon administration is bringing all this experience to a grim
climax. The present government has dashed all liberal
dreams of the war being "phased out" from above, and instead has provoked a wider war which could well escalate
into nuclear attacks on Vietnam and China. The same government has designed a war against black liberation at home
through military attacks on the Panthers and "benign neglect" for black people in general. Incendiary propaganda,
conspiracy indictments, and killings in Berkeley, Santa Barbara, and Kent State have been the main official reaction to
alienated white youth.

We live in a constitutional crisis. The ruling powers have

usurped power not only from the people but from their own Senators and Congressmen, to a point where only the President and his military-industrial advisory board know where the next war will begin. Nixon is even said to have requested a Rand Corporation study of the means to declare martial law and suspend the 1972 elections.

We must react immediately to this crisis, if only to delay the escalation and expose it further to the American people. The unprecedented student strike beginning in New Haven is likely to continue and widen by fall. A revolutionary Continental Congress this summer and the projected September demonstration at the United Nations will mobilize people here and abroad against the menace our government has become.

But the crisis will not be solved by the election of a few more "liberals," nor by campaigns, even strikes, against a particular policy. The political history of the 1960s is one chapter after another of frustrated reform efforts. But in our failures to make the system work these last ten years, we have learned a most important lesson: *that ordinary people can and do make history.* Outpourings of disruptive energy have caused these reform campaigns—the sit-ins leading to the Voting Rights Law, the resistance leading to the McCarthy campaign, the trashing of ROTC buildings leading to the university "reconstitution" movement just this Spring. And the same disruptive energy has continued to mount despite all efforts to "contain" it within reformism. Taking this observation as a starting point and looking ahead into the seventies, we should look for a revolutionary strategy in the location and direction of this popular energy. The process of revolution takes shape in the way people are moving against the structures oppressing them.

First, we need no longer believe that the protest of the sixties involved only a marginal lunatic fringe. There is no new silent majority maturing to replace the old. In the black community, according to *Time,* over half the people are positively oriented toward the Panthers (and much larger numbers of the young than the old). Among whites, where the "lunatic fringe" analysis is more popular, radicalism also shows strength—even in the polls of the Establishment. One of the best known polls, conducted by *Fortune* in 1968, showed 750,000 students who "should know better" identifying with the New Left, while another two or three million constituted a supportive base. "This particular younger generation is by all odds the most interesting to come along in U.S. history," *Fortune* concedes, ". . . it will shortly preside over the revolutionary changes that await us." Now that millions of students across America are shutting down their schools in protest against the war and repression, can we any longer doubt our vast potential numbers?

Nor can we believe any longer that we are simply going through a "generation gap." That shallow theory locates the source of social conflict in failures of communication. Ever since the beginnings of protest ten years ago we have been told that radicalism is a part of the cycle of history, that today's radical undergraduate becomes a mellow liberal at thirty and a responsible citizen at forty. But after a decade this gap seems as wide as the one between Earth and Mars.

The phrase "generation gap" is a euphemism for the new location of class struggle. We are not a lunatic fringe; we are a New People rising from the ruins of the American empire. Not surprisingly, journals like *Fortune* and *Time* have difficulty coming to this conclusion because that would destroy their game; they would then have to point to themselves, to their system of international capitalism, to find the causes of the revolt.

Modern American capitalism is dooming itself in the very process of its own development. Its current form arose out of the Great Depression and World War II when private enterprise, the State, and the military merged in a centralized structure of power with the world's most advanced level of technology. The result was a total breakdown of traditional images and values, a rupture of the material base of society away from its cultural superstructure, and a permanent breakdown of control over the young.

Private property and puritan morality, while still endorsed by dinosaurs like the Nixon family, became obsolete concepts in this new situation. Enterprising entrepreneurs were replaced by conforming organization men. For the first time in history, most people felt insured against hunger and were able to imagine a less competitive life, a life beyond scarcity.

Militarism and racism, too, suddenly became obsolete values in the postwar world. Warned by successive Presidents that the arms race was ultimately irrational and that white racism was unallowable in the new world of nations, we watched while the government permitted these problems to become more dangerous with each year.

The chief contradiction in America is between a moribund, decadent system and all those people with a stake in the future. Just at the moment when the system seems most exhausted in its potential to solve the problems it has created, it gives birth to a permanently restless generation with the freedom to be idealistic.

It is not simply "internal" changes in American capitalism that bring on the crisis, however. For those changes are largely designed to cope with the worldwide revolutionary process unleashed in the postwar period. As the chief pillar of the free world, the United States is being assaulted on all sides by anti-colonial and socialist revolution. As the vanguard of counterrevolution, the United States is forced to invest ever greater sums in "defense," to neglect even the most modest domestic needs, and to become barbaric in its violence. The image of idealism has passed from the American government (which in World War II could wear an anti-fascist face, and as late as 1960 could announce a "peace corps") to the rebels of the world, including the blacks at home. This revolutionary upsurge opens the eyes of Americans daily, not only to the role of our government but to the idealism and optimism of people rising from their knees the world over. The world has changed from a one-dimensional "American Century" (1945) to a two-dimensional world of empire and revolution. Everyone is confronted with the message: you are either part of the problem or part of the solution.

Virtually every young person in America feels this situation in some way. They know, first, that the United States has the technical ability to create economic security and a better life for everyone in the world and, second, that a new world is taking shape in which the competition, racism, and corruption of the generation now in power will have no place.

That is why the rise of an American student movement in the last decade is a revolutionary, not a routine, event. In fact, during its rise to empire the United States was never plagued by "student unrest" on the scale now being experienced. To find any parallels one would have to look at other countries where student movements have been indicators of fundamental change. Instead of seeing the American youth revolt as a "last gasp" by romantic diehards, as social scientists and journalists often did in the sixties, it would be better understood as the harbinger of a great change. The breakdown of the social order is first and always felt by the young, the students, the people who must plan for the future.

What this means, for the time being, is that "youth" is more important than "economic class" in analyzing the American struggle. A generation ago it was the industrial working class that felt the shock of industrial change most severely. But since the war, young people of all classes have been the chief victims bearing the burden of the expanding empire. Most young people are in school or in the army or are unemployed. They are tied as technicians, propagandists, service or manual workers to an imperialism that destroys their values and taxes and drafts them for impossible wars. When we see that the youth revolt is international, occurring around the same issues in West Germany, Italy, France, and all the "advanced countries" linked to the United States, we see that the crisis truly is one of a decaying global imperialism.

With the passage of time, with the further decay of the American empire, the discontent now felt most by youth will spread with them wherever they go to work or live. In the long run, then, the alienation of youth may become an alienation of *the whole people.* In a period of collapsing empire, those with a solid stake in the status quo gradually become fewer and fewer. In the Panthers phrase, the ultimate struggle becomes one "between the people and the pigs."

The present official authorities are dinosaurs. Although they are in power, they are fast becoming extinct. Faced with Richard Nixon, Spiro Agnew, Ronald Reagan and Julius Hoffman, young people sense immediately that dialogue is as impossible with them as with one's ancestors. These rulers face a real inheritance crisis. Even in their own social class, they see their sons and daughters on the barricades, smoking pot or freaking out. They sense that they have no future. Defensively they speak of a "silent majority." Like General Custer they are both dangerous and impotent: *they can kill but never win.*

Seen in this framework, Nixon and Agnew look more like the dangerous impostors they are. They are living fossils, with roots mostly among the most decayed and aging elements of the population. In their case, power has come unhinged from authority. Their power lies in the machinery they use to tax, draft, and brutalize the people. But they lack the consent of the governed in the ghettos, colleges, and high schools. Losing control over the conscripted army, they turn increasingly to professional Gestapo-types at home and abroad. At best, they are ruling half a society—and the aging half at that.

One reason they seem so powerful is that their opposition —the liberal Democrats—has been so thoroughly discredited. Unlike the radicals and the conservatives, the liberals have no program or ideology to make sense of this crisis. When respectable Yale hosted a May Day rally for the Black Panthers, a university official there bemoaned the fact that no political force existed "between the Chicago Seven and Spiro T. Agnew." This particular liberal should have no trouble understanding.the crisis of liberalism since his background is in the Department of Defense. It is precisely this marriage of postwar liberalism to America's basic institutions that has prevented liberalism from advancing a meaningful alternative.

Conceivably liberalism will be revived, if only because Nixon and Agnew are so weak. A new liberal program— withdrawal from Vietnam, the placing of poverty funds under community control, cuts in the military budget, new legal rights for students and young people, legalization of dope, etc.—would have a mass constituency in the seventies. But liberalism by definition has little will to fight the system, and with the Democratic Party controlled by labor and party hacks, it has no electoral machinery. Moreover, even assuming a revived liberalism, even assuming a President John Lindsay or Ramsey Clark or Kingman Brewster, the introduction of palliatives might only inflame rather than calm the social crisis. The menacing attitude of New York's police and conservative citizens toward Lindsay is only a taste of what the military-industrial complex would have in store for a reform-minded president. Even the threat of reform is enough to mobilize conservative power for a showdown. In a worsening crisis, militant counterrevolutionaries would move to rout the liberals through ballots or bullets. Instead of hoping for a political saviour or a revival of the liberal politics that failed in the sixties, we see in our protest movement the seeds from which to create our own future institutions of government. We should put less hope in machinery that has proven itself ineffective, and begin creating new machinery to meet our needs.

If we look at any revolutionary movement, we see that it evolves through three overlapping stages. The first is *protest,* in which people petition their rulers for specific policy changes. When the level of protest becomes massive, the rulers begin to apply pressures to suppress it. This in turn drives the people toward the second stage, *resistance,* in which they begin to contest the legitimacy of the rulers. As this conflict sharpens, resistance leads to a *liberation* phase in which the ruling structure disintegrates and new institutions are established by the people. America in the sixties experienced primarily the protest phase, but resistance has already become commonplace among the blacks and the young. Temporary periods of liberation have even been achieved—as when students occupied Columbia University for one week and learned they could create new relationships and govern themselves. Of course, these experiences only provide a glimpse of liberation as long as the government has sufficient police power to restore university officials to office.

In the resistance phase it becomes necessary to lay plans for defeating the police and building a new society. It is a time of showdown in which the government will either crush the resistance and restore its own power, or undergo constant failure, eroding its own base to a very dangerous point. Because it challenges the legitimacy of the way things are ordered, resistance acquires the responsibility of proposing and creating new arrangements.

The general goals of American revolutionaries are not too difficult to state. We want to abolish a private property system which, in its drive for new markets, benefits only a few while colliding violently with the aspirations of people all over the world. We want a transformation in which the masses of people, organized around their own needs, create a new, humane, and participatory system.

What is less clear is the kind of structural rearrangement that will be required to achieve these goals. A radical movement always begins to create within itself the structures that will eventually form the basis of the new society. So it is necessary to look at the structure of motion-now-in-progress to understand what must be destroyed and what must be built. We need a new Continental Congress to explore where our institutions have failed and to declare new principles for organizing our society.

The first principle of any new arrangement is *self-determination for our internal colonies.* In the seventies the Third World revolutions will sharpen not only on other continents but here inside the United States. The black ghettos are a chain of islands forming a single domestic colony. The same is true of the Puerto Rican people struggling for independence in San Juan, New York, and Chicago; the Chicano people of the Southwest; and the Asians and Indians struggling in their small urban and rural communities. The concept of "integration," which so dominated consciousness in the sixties, is now blinding most people to the new reality of self-determination. Underlying the desire for integration is the even deeper belief that America is "one nation, indivisible." It seems unthinkable that this country might literally be broken up into self-determining parts (nations on the same land), yet that is more or less what is evolving. The failure of the United States to make progress in the areas of education, jobs, housing and land reform here at home, the constant recourse to repressive violence at a time when the "revolution of rising expectations" is nowhere stronger than in America, can only make Third World people turn toward independence.

The second principle of rearrangement should be the creation of *Free Territories in the Mother Country.* Already we are seen as alien and outside White Civilization by those in power. It is necessary for us to create amidst the falling ruins of this empire a new, alternative way of life more in harmony with the interests of the world's people.

Abbie is a pioneer in this struggle, but so far "Woodstock Nation" is purely cultural, a state of mind shared by thousands of young people. The next stage is to make this "Woodstock Nation" an organized reality with its own revolutionary institutions and, starting immediately, with roots in its own territory. At the same time, the need to overcome our inbred, egoistic, male, middle-class character, and especially to create solidarity with Third World struggles, has to become a foremost part of our consciousness.

The new people in white America are clustering in ghetto communities of their own: Berkeley, Haight-Ashbury, Isla Vista, Madison, Ann Arbor, rural Vermont, the East Village, the Upper West Side. These communities, often created on the edge of universities, are not the bohemian enclaves of ten years ago. Those places, like Greenwich Village and North Beach, developed when the alienated were still a marginal group. Now millions of young people have nowhere else to go. They live cheaply in their own communities; go to school or to various free universities; study crafts and new skills; learn self-defense; read the underground press; go to demonstrations. The hard core of these new territories is the lumpen-bourgeoisie, dropouts from the American way of life. But in any such community there is a cross-section of people whose needs overlap. In Berkeley, for example, there are students, street people, left-liberals, and blacks, together constituting a radical political majority of the city. Communities like this are nearly as alien to police and "solid citizens" as are the black ghettos.

The importance of these communities is that they add a dimension of territory, of real physical space, to the consciousness of those within. The final break with mainstream America comes, after all, when you literally *cannot* live there, when it becomes imperative to live more closely with "your own kind."

Until recently people dropped out in their minds, or into tiny bohemian enclaves. Now they drop out collectively, into territory. In this situation feelings of individual isolation are replaced by a common consciousness of large numbers sharing the same needs. It is possible to go anywhere in America and find the section of town inhabited by the dropouts, the freaks, and the radicals. It is a nationwide network of people with the same oppression, the same institutions and language, the same music, the same styles, the same needs and grievances: the very essence of a new society taking root and growing up in the framework of the old.

The ruling class views this pattern with growing alarm. They analyze places like Berkeley as "red zones" like the ones they attempt to destroy in Vietnam. Universities and urban renewal agencies everywhere are busy moving into and destroying our communities, breaking them up physically, escalating the rents, tearing down cheap housing and replacing it with hotels, convention centers and university buildings. Politicians declare a "crime wave" (dope) and double the police patrols. Tens of thousands of kids are harassed, busted, moved on.

In every great revolution there have been such "liberated zones" where radicalism was most deeply rooted, where people tried to meet their own needs while fighting off the official governing power. If there is revolutionary change inside the Mother Country, it will originate in the Berkeleys and Madisons, where people are similarly rooted and where we are defending ourselves against constantly growing aggression.

The concept of Free Territories does *not* mean local struggles for "community control" in the traditional sense —battles that are usually limited to electoral politics and maneuvering for control of funds from the state or federal government. Our struggles will largely ignore or resist outside administration and instead build and defend our own institutions.

Nor does the concept mean withdrawal into comfortable radical enclaves remote from the rest of America. The Territories should be centers from which a challenge to the whole Establishment is mounted.

Such Free Territories would have four common points of identity:

First, *they will be utopian centers of new cultural experiment.* "All Power to the Imagination" has real meaning for people experiencing the breakdown of our decadent culture. In the Territories all traditional social relations—starting with the oppression of women—would be overturned. The nuclear family would be replaced by a mixture of communes, extended families, children's centers, and new schools. Women would have their own communes and organizations. Work would be redefined as a task done for the community and controlled by the workers and people affected. Drugs would be commonly used as a means of deepening self-awareness. Urban structures would be destroyed, to be replaced with parks, closed streets, expanded backyards inside blocks, and a village atmosphere in general would be encouraged. Education would be reorganized along revolutionary lines, with children really participating. Music and art would be freed from commercial control and widely performed in the community. At all levels the goal would be to eliminate egoism, competition, and aggression from our personalities.

Second, *the Territories will be internationalist. Cultural experiment without internationalism is privilege; internationalism without cultural revolution is false consciousness.* People in our Territories would act as citizens of an international community, an obstructive force inside imperialism. Solidarity committees to aid all Third World struggles would be in constant motion. Each Territory would see itself as an "international city." The flags, music, and culture of other countries and other liberation movements would permeate the Territory.

Travel and "foreign relations" with other nations would be commonplace. All imperialist institutions (universities, draft boards, corporations) in or near the Territory would be under constant siege. An underground railroad would exist to support revolutionary fugitives.

Third, *the Territories will be centers of constant confrontation, battlefronts inside the Mother Country*. Major institutions such as universities and corporations would be under constant pressure either to shut down or to serve the community. The occupying police would be systematically opposed. Stores would be pressured to transform themselves into community-serving institutions. Tenant unions would seek to break the control of absentee landlords and to transform local housing into communal shelter. There would be continual defiance of tax, draft and drug laws. Elected officials would serve the community or be challenged by parallel structures of power. Protest campaigns of national importance, such as the anti-war movement, would be initiated from within the Territories. The constant process of confrontation would not only weaken the control of the power structure, but would serve also to create a greater sense of our own identity, our own possibilities.

Fourth, *they will be centers of survival and self-defense*. The Territories would include free medical and legal services, child-care centers, drug clinics, crash pads, instant communication networks, job referral and welfare centers—all the basic services to meet people's needs as they struggle and change. Training in physical self-defense and the use of weapons would become commonplace as fascism and vigilantism increase.

Insurgent, even revolutionary, activity will occur outside as well as inside the Territories. Much of it already is within institutions (workplaces, army bases, schools, even "behind enemy lines" in the government). But the Territories will be like models or beacons to those who struggle within these institutions, and the basic tension will tend always to occur between the authorities and the Territories pulling people out of the mainstream.

The Territories will establish once and for all the polarized nature of the Mother Country. No longer will Americans be able to think comfortably of themselves as a homogeneous society with a few extremists at the fringes. No longer will politicians and administrators be able to feel confident in their power to govern the entire United States. Beneath the surface of official power, the Territories will be giving birth to new centers of power.

In the foreseeable future, Free Territories will have to operate with a strategy of "dual power"—that is, people would stay within the legal structure of the United States, involuntarily if for no other reason, while building new forms with which to replace that structure. The thrust of these new forms will be resistance against illegitimate outside authority, and constant attempts at self-government.

Mother Country radicalism will have its unique organizational forms. Revolutionary movements have turned toward the concept of a centralized, disciplined, nationally-based "vanguard" party that leads a variety of mass organizations representing specific interests (women, labor, students, etc.). This organizational form is logical where people are already disciplined by their situation (as in a large factory) or where the goal is "state power." But it is not so clear that such an organizational form is necessary—at least now—for Mother Country radicalism. Certainly the excessive individualism and egoism, which dominate the culture of young people, must be overcome if we are going to survive, much less make a revolution. But the organizational form must be consistent with the kind of revolution we are trying to make. For that reason *the collective* in some form should be the basis of revolutionary organization.

A revolutionary collective would not be like the organizations to which we give part-time attachment today, the kind where we attend meetings, "participate" by speaking and voting, and perhaps learn how to use a mimeograph machine. The collectives would be much more about our *total* lives. Instead of developing our talents within schools and other Establishment institutions, we would develop them primarily within our own collectives. In these groups we would learn politics, self-defense, languages, ecology, medical skills, industrial techniques—everything that helps people grow toward independence. Thus the collectives would not be just organizational weapons to use against the Establishment, but organs fostering the development of revolutionary people.

The emphasis in this kind of organization is on power from below. It begins with a distrust of highly centralized or elite-controlled organizations. But we should also recognize that decentralization can degenerate into anarchy and tribalism. Collectives must stress the need for unity and cooperation, especially on projects that require large numbers or when common interests are threatened. We should seek the advantages of coordinated power while avoiding the problem of an established hierarchy. A network of collectives can act as the "revolutionary council" of a given Territory and a network of such councils can unite the Territories across the United States. In addition to such political coordination, the Territories can be united through the underground press and culture, through conferences and constant travel.

Finally and above all, the concept of Free Territories does not imply that the youth movement is already "revolutionary," except in its potential. Free Territories are only a form in which the struggle goes on. Both the "student movement" and the "youth culture" still must deal with the permeation of *white, male, middle-class attitudes.* Neither students on strike nor stoned freaks in the street constitute a real revolutionary force. There must be still more transformation of our character on all levels. Male chauvinism must be overthrown in the political movement and the rock culture; individualism and egoism must be replaced by a collective spirit; narrow, middle-class demands for privilege must be replaced by demands in the interest of the taxpaying masses.

Such a transformation might seem impossible in the Western cultural context of "rugged individualism," comic-book cowboys, and Dick Tracy. If our generation has produced one classic political type, it is Macho-Man, the swaggering, aggressive political or cultural hero. This personality type is pernicious to revolutionary change because it is driven by the same status needs that pervade the larger society. Not only does this ego-tripping contradict revolutionary values, but it becomes suicidal in a period of approaching fascism. In a time of resistance and extra-legal activity, with agents everywhere, there is no outlet for those who must tell the world (or at least their "chicks") of their feats. We need a "revolution in the revolution" to deal with this continuing arrogance. The most burning need for a change in our attitudes lies in our relationship to Third World Liberation struggles.

The creation of Free Territories in the Mother Country is not separate from the national liberation battles of Third World people. The Territories are a way to prepare for the vast international uprising which will be the next American Revolution.

We must not follow the chauvinist path taken by the left in other colonial periods. Our support for black liberation must be unconditional. We must begin by making it clear that there will be no racism and no racist escapism in the peace movement or in "Woodstock Nation." If we are serious about becoming new men and women, free of the bloody legacy of white American civilization, then we have the responsibility of becoming the first white people in history to live beyond racial definitions of interest. There is something racist about "Woodstock Nation"—not the familiar racism of George Wallace, but an attitude of distance that comes from living in the most comfortable oppression the world has ever known. We are constantly in danger of escaping into a cultural revolution of our own, a tiny island of post-scarcity hedonism, pacifism, and fantasy far from the blood and fire of the Third World.

White radicals can follow the path of their own legitimate revolution, however, without abandoning the Vietnamese and the blacks. In fact we cannot realize our own needs without the destruction of the same colonial system that brutalizes the Third World. We are at one end of a line of resistance whose other end is rooted in black America and the Third World. Young white people today, whether working-class or middle-class, are the first privileged generation with no real interest in inheriting the capitalist system. We have experienced its affluence and know that life involves far more than suburban comfort. We know further that this system contains its own self-destruct: racism, exploitation, and militarism lead nowhere in the contemporary world but to war and waste. As we look out over the top of imperialism we should be able to see that our true allies are those who live below and beyond its privilege, the wretched of the earth.

Certainly there is a gap between the children of affluence and the children of squalor. Our need for a new life style, for women's liberation, for the transformation of work, for a new environment and educational system, cannot be described in the rhetoric of Third World revolution where poverty, exploitation, and fascist violence are the immediate crisis. We cannot be black; nor can our needs be entrusted to a Third World vanguard of any kind.

But our destiny and possible liberation cannot be separated from the Third World vanguards. The change toward which we are inevitably moving is one in which the white world yields power and resources to an insistent humanity. There is no escape—either into rural communes or existential mysticism—from this dynamic of world confrontation. By our deeds each day we are determining what role, if any, we will have in the world's future. What we have and have not done, for Bobby, and for Cuba, and for Vietnam, measures exactly our stature in the new world being created.

Some will cry that this cosmic formulation denies the issue of priorities. How shall it be settled whether to work first against racism, or the war, or male supremacy, or the production speed-up? Historically the white left has argued that colonial liberation should wait for socialist revolution or be submerged in a black-white working-class coalition. In the same vein, some Panthers today argue that the women's movement should wait until blacks are liberated. Special interests seem constantly in danger of being betrayed, and so we fragment into groups with particular, immediate priorities.

At first this fragmentation appears hopeless. But the fact that so many different people are moving at once for their own liberation suggests an inspiring possibility. *We are living in a time of universal desire for a new social order. a time when total revolution is on the agenda:* not a limited and particular "revolution" for national identity here, for the working class there, for women here—but *for all of humanity* to build a new, freer way of life by sharing the world's vast resources equally and fraternally. The world's people are so interdependent that a strike for freedom anywhere creates vibrations everywhere. The American empire itself is so worldwide in scope that humanity has for the first time not only a common spirit but a common enemy. Through their particular struggles, more and more revolutionaries see the possibilities of the "new man" envisioned by Che Guevara. Formed in an international upheaval, such a human being would be universal in character for the first time in history. To become such a whole person in the present means fighting not only around immediate self-interest but against all levels of oppression at once.

It is in this context that priorities, especially the priority of Bobby Seale's trial, should be understood. Vanguards will be discovered in action, and priorities will be created where total showdowns between the status quo and revolution appear. Bobby's case, and the repression of the Panthers generally, embodies just such a showdown. Bobby and the Panthers were the first to raise the battle cry of liberation inside America, the first black revolutionary party with an internationalist perspective, the first to threaten imperialism totally from within. The U.S. government certainly sees the Panthers this way; that is why it is attempting, through Bobby's trial, to demonstrate that genocide awaits all who rebel. All those who value their own liberation must go with the Panthers and Bobby as they become symbols of humanity making a time-honored stand: Freedom or Death.